MW01491405

JAGDSTAFFEL 356

JAGDSTAFFEL 356

The Story of a
German Fighter Squadron

BY
M. E. KÄHNERT

Translated from the German by
CLAUD W. SYKES

CASEMATE
Philadelphia & Oxford

This edition of *Jagdstaffel 356* is published in
the United States of America and Great Britain in 2014 by
CASEMATE
908 Darby Road, Havertown, PA 19083
and
10 Hythe Bridge Street, Oxford, OX1 2EW

 *A Greenhill Book*

ISBN 978-1-61200-144-9
Digital Edition: ISBN 978-1-61200-145-6

Cataloging-in-publication data is available from the Library of Congress
and the British Library.

Printed and bound in the United States of America.

For a complete list of Casemate titles please contact:

CASEMATE PUBLISHERS (US)
Telephone (610) 853-9131, Fax (610) 853-9146
E-mail: casemate@casematepublishing.com

CASEMATE PUBLISHERS (UK)
Telephone (01865) 241249, Fax (01865) 794449
E-mail: casemate-uk@casematepublishing.co.uk

Contents

ILLUSTRATIONS

PUBLISHING HISTORY

Jagdstaffel 356 was originally published in Germany in 1933 by Union Verlagsgesellschaft, Stuttgart. This new edition is reproduced complete and unabridged from the first English translation which was published by John Hamilton Ltd, ca 1935, in London.

Although the author of *Jagdstaffel 356* has obviously given this Jagdstaffel a fictitious number and changed the names of the pilots composing it, the incidents related in this book have the genuine ring of truth and will be recognised as facts by anyone who has had experience flying on the Western Front or who has studied it since. Whatever its real number may have been, Jagdstaffel 356 undoubtedly fought in the air over Flanders in 1918.

Chapter I

They all kept step. There were eight pilots, headed by the Staffel-leader and the divisional chaplain, and then the long ranks of mechanics. They marched in a slow, measured time which was dictated to them by the band playing the solemn, long-drawn strains of Chopin's Funeral March.

"Where are we going to get a band from?" Steffen had asked. There was reason in his question, because a Jagdstaffel is an insignificant group in comparison with the thousands of other larger formations. What do eleven pilots and sixty-nine mechanics count in the scheme of things? They cannot and must not allow themselves any such luxuries.

"We'll ring up Captain M. of the artillery," the chief replied. "He'll help us out."

Of course they got their band. "We must keep in with the airmen," thought Captain M. "And it'll be a good lesson, too, for my musicians when they realise that not everyone gets buried in a mass grave in war. Besides, we've all got to help each other."

The procession wound its way slowly along the shell-scarred road.

"He'll never get another drink;
In the grave it's cold, I think.

9

> Was that fellow quite insane
> To climb into an aeroplane?"

they all hummed through tightly pressed lips. No good getting soft. Your turn today; mine, perhaps, tomorrow. So they kept on muttering the silly doggerel.

Two comrades had fallen in aerial combat. Their bodies were found on the German side of the lines. Two coffins were fashioned; wreaths were plaited. Messages of sympathy came from the neighbouring Staffels, and their own machines carried black streamers. They had some hankering for the forms and ceremonies, for the War did not eradicate the traditions of civilian life, which included beautiful and solemn funerals, and they had all the facilities for them. But, for Heaven's sake, no sentimentality! Sad enough when pilots get shot down, but that sort of thing happens on the other side of the lines too! And the more such casualties that occur on the German side, the greater the honour won by the Germans!

In any case scouting pilots do not fight men; they fight the enemy's machines. Or, to put it better, machine fights machine. It is a knightly affair, not a mere butchery. The methods of destruction employed by a few thousand airmen must naturally differ from those used by the millions in the trenches. Scouting pilots have their unwritten laws, which the men on the ground cannot have.

And now they stood by the gaping graves. Every now and then they cast searching glances at the horizon, where their trained eyes picked out the cloudlets of the anti-aircraft batteries at the nearby front. But there was no enemy in sight; for the moment, at least, there was peace in the sky.

The chaplain spoke. His words were good but simple, for in those days when millions departed this life without a blessing from heaven, any attempt at consolation was of doubtful value. The volleys resounded; the band struck up: "I had a comrade." That went home to them all, because they were all comrades—each for all and all for each.

But these ten pilots and their twenty-six-year-old leader and their sixty-nine mechanics seldom thought about such things. They were a unit, or rather, a unity, and now a gap had been torn in their unity. "Comrades in the air and comrades on the ground," was the chief's slogan, and they remembered it when each of them threw three handfuls of earth into the grave. Earth is dirt, as everything is dirt. But earth is also something sacred. May our two dead comrades sleep well, they wished, and on the Day of Judgment may they be forgiven all their sins! And may the same forgiveness be accorded also to the thousands of comrades who await the end of all things in the huge cemetery here!

The Jagdstaffel had good quarters. It was housed in an old Flanders country seat, with thick, kindly walls which still remained unharmed, and capacious buildings around it to accommodate all their men and materials. There was ample space for hangars for the brown Fokkers, workshops, petrol and oil stores and garages on the surrounding meadowland, while the aerodrome was not inconvenienced by too many tall trees.

The pilots sat at their evening meal in the mess. In this Staffel there was no difference made between the officer pilots and those belonging to "other ranks." It was only right for all the pilots to sit at the same table, because they were all there for the same purpose, which was to win honour and fame for the Staffel. The small, slender lieutenant sat at the head, and the others were seated in order of seniority. But two chairs were empty that day.

The orderly bent over to the chief and made an announcement. Nine pairs of eyes turned eagerly towards the door.

The "new man" entered with soldierly steps, stood to attention in front of the chief and reported himself with the words: "Pilot Hamann, transferred from the Jagdstaffel School to Jagdstaffel 356, sir!" Then they all stood up. The chief inclined his head slightly and shook the newcomer by the hand. "Staffel-leader Olden," he answered. "Thank you."

Names buzzed through the air.

"Hamann, how old are you?"

"Seventeen, sergeant."

"Man alive!"

An empty chair had found an occupant, and on the morrow the other gap would be filled too.

They all knew that this hour was the most important one of the new man's service with the Staffel. He had to make answer to all sorts of good-natured but personal questions, for it was their task to give him an unmistakable demonstration of their spirit of comradeship. There was no room for the boastful or conceited fellow in their midst.

The newcomer could drink well enough; it was to be hoped that his flying was up to the same standard. No, they did not want to probe the depths of his soul, but that was the hour when he had to give them some revelation of his personality. He would have to show that he could fit into their community, and the thanks he would receive would be the friendship of them all. They were still boys—most of them Bavarian boys; few were over twenty, but all were hard-bitten, experienced and free of illusions.

With bright eyes the youth scanned the trophies adorning the walls of the mess. There were broken propellers, streamers of leadership, numbers removed from the wings of enemy machines.

"Well, tell us something about your own experiences as a pilot," said Kussin, leaning his arms comfortably on the table.

"You there," called out the chief, "twelve marks fine for bad manners!"

The chief led a Jagdstaffel and had won the *Pour le Mérite* Order for shooting down 36 enemy machines, but he was only twenty-six years old. As he had to be the educator of his Staffel as well as its leader, he could not help employing drastic methods sometimes. On the table beside him there was a large book, in which all offences against good behaviour were entered.

Kussin groaned as he extracted his wallet, but he knew he would see value for his money. One day when the Staffel went off to Ghent or Brussels on a community leave, all the money collected in fines would be spent riotously. "Comrades in the air—comrades on the ground!"

Mechanic Huber tiptoed across to Olden. "I've packed the lieutenant's and the sergeant's things, sir," he announced. "Will you please tell me where to send them, sir?"

They were all silent. Baum stood up. "I'll attend to that, chief; don't worry."

They let him go out with the orderly without further ado. They knew that Baum—the little pilot with the thick black hair and the eyes of a fanatic—had been a very close friend of the two dead men. Their eyes wandered to the chair which was still empty, and then to the one occupied by the new man.

Hamann felt that this was the moment when they expected something from him—when they wanted him to show them in some way or other that he was worthy to be of their community. But how to do it? What experience of life had he gained in his seventeen years? Years of school, voluntary enlistment and training. Training? Yes, it was training that told.

LIEUTENANT
OLDEN

CHAPTER II

A thick haze of tobacco hung over the small round table. Someone had found some English cigarettes somewhere, and there was no doubt they were better than the rose-leaf tobacco. With them there was French wine, and the combination formed an excellent basis for talking shop.

"Strange that so many cavalrymen transfer to flying," said Rom. "Then they get a shock when they find their training doesn't carry them through. Crashed machines and broken backs are the results. How did you find things in your time, Kussin?"

"In Ghent we all had to pass the pilots' special active service tests, and there weren't so many crashes, but about fifty percent of my pals who trained at home broke their necks," was the reply.

"And then there are a good many fellows who think that you've as good as insured your life if you get put on one of those big fat furniture vans known as bombing machines," opined Steffen.

"Rot! The casualty lists show that losses are comparatively lightest in the scouts. But anyone who tries to preach that ———"

Olden rose and turned to the new man. "General Höppner doesn't want to see that English captive balloon round Ypres way going up much longer. You'd better come and have a look at it with me tomorrow; perhaps we'll bag it, and perhaps we won't. By the way, there's a reward if you shoot it down! Good night, gentlemen!"

That was official. They all rose. "Good night, Herr Lieutenant!"

"Oh, yes, Höppner—Ghent, of course!" Hamann smiled.

"What! Did you meet him there? Tell us!" one of them called out to him.

They leant their arms on their table and stretched their bodies across it, for the black fine-book had vanished.

"Well, in Ghent there were seventy-eight of us aviation pupils living in the Chateau Rouge, and it was fine. They put us through it, but we flew fast types of war machines and furnished the anti-enemy aircraft patrol."

"We know all that," muttered Rom. "Just the same as it was in our time."

"Did the cavalry officers go on wearing their old uniforms in your time?" asked the new man. "It looked really funny to see a lot of Uhlans, cuirassiers and dragoons as pilots!"

"Of course they did," replied Rom, "and we poor infantry privates spent our extra pay on togging ourselves out in the maddest sets of uniforms. Breeches that wide!" he indicated a most incredible width with his two hands, "and tunics that fitted you like a glove. . . ."

". . . And silk caps that perched on one side of your head, that made such a lovely crinkle," Hamann exclaimed in the midst of the joyous laughter. "It was one of those caps that was my undoing!"

They pushed their chairs up close so as not to lose one of the speaker's words.

"So one day His Excellency von Höppner rolls up for an inspection. Everyone's trembling at the knees, including the chief. The next morning finds us seventy-eight pupils drawn up on the aerodrome—cleaner and tidier than you could have thought possible. The forty officers in the front rank, the N.C.O.s—about thirty of them—in the second, and we eight privates in the third.

THE MACHINES OF A JAGDSTAFFEL, READY TO TAKE OFF

"We got our orders: 'On the knee!' and then we waited a full half-hour. We went on waiting until my knees were numb. At last a car came along. We could see the gleam of gold lace from afar—and so much gold lace could only mean a general. It was his High and Mightiness himself. We eight privates were ready to take off in the wobbliest death-traps ever seen on an aerodrome if only the general was merciful to us!

"The officer pupils got some polite words from him, and he was quite jovial with the second rank. Then we privates in the third one saw the old man's erect figure, with an ice-grey moustache and piercing eyes under bristling brows and lots of red and gold about him—in short, a proper general!"

His eight listeners were highly delighted for they remembered their own encounters with generals.

"His Excellency approached," continued Hamann with a sigh. "The other seven pilots from the ranks had the Iron Cross, because they'd all been at the front, but I had nothing but half a year's home training behind me. The general asked the other seven in a friendly voice where they got their Iron Crosses, but there was an undertone of irritation in his friendliness. The aerodrome commander was pale with excitement as he walked a pace behind his guest.

"Then my turn came. 'How long have you served?' he asked. 'Eight months, Your Excellency,' I replied. 'Profession in civilian life?' 'Secondary schoolboy, Your Excellency,' 'Why's your cap so much on one side of your head? You look like a robber chief.' I was just going to adjust that beautiful, expensive silk cap when the thunderstorm broke. 'Keep your hands down when I'm speaking to you,' he bellowed."

The eight listeners were so highly delighted that they failed to notice the blush of embarrassment on Hamann's face.

"You see, that's the trouble when a chief gets his crowd too perfect. It was all too clean and tidy on our aerodrome, and an inspection which reveals nothing wrong is no inspection at all. 'Captain,' said the general, 'this volunteer looks like a civilian in disguise. Uniforms such as he is wearing tend to have a very bad effect on army discipline. Can the fellow even fly?' 'Your Excellency,' says the captain, 'he was sent on to us after a complete training course at home!'

"During this brief conversation my teeth were chattering, and shivers went down my spine. 'Get into a machine,' says the general, 'any type you like, and let me see you fly a round of the aerodrome.'

" 'At Your Excellency's orders!' I shouted with the last remnants of my ebbing strength, and buzzed off to the hangars with two mechanics. 'What machine had I better take?' I asked as we ran along. 'Try the Albatros D. III, that spinning one-seater,' says the experienced mechanic, 'and take off like a gentleman. The wind's blowing in the direction of our gold-laced guest, so fly up to him with an open throttle, pull your machine up sharp to 500 metres just as you get to him; keep on flying with your stick against your tummy until you're flying head downwards. Then cut your engine, and you've done a loop! Then you can spin down and report: 'Orders carried out, Your Excellency.' So I climbed in and they buckled my belt. Ready? Ready! All clear! Hals and Beinbruch!"

The eight listeners had almost forgotten the contents of their glasses.

"The machine was wonderful. I didn't fly it; it flew me. I made up my mind to show him what real flying was. My take-off was beautiful, but I held my breath before that loop, because it was my first. I just pulled the stick up to my tummy, and kept on pulling until I was hanging head downwards. I pulled away till I saw the sky again, and then something biffed my face hard. It gave me another biff, and I was in such a blue funk that I switched off the engine, whereupon the machine stood on her tail, sideslipped, slewed round to one side—and I found myself going down in a spin! The ground seemed to be reaching up to me, and it looked very hard.

"But anyhow I'd done a loop—my first loop! I put the controls to central; the Albatros responded at once and came out of her spin.

A German Artillery Observation Machine

I switched on again when I was about the height of the hangars, slid up to the landing T., and made an elegant landing ten paces away from the general."

The eight listeners drew long breaths of relief.

"The biffs I got were from two screw-nuts on the switchboard, which the mechanics had forgotten to remove. I reported: 'Orders carried out, Your Excellency,' but he was red in the face, and not exactly with pleasure, I sensed. 'Man alive, are you quite dotty? I'll give you three days' cells! Captain, put him under arrest at once. I'll punish you with three days' cells for frivolous risk to state property and your own life!'

"Well, I fetched up in the guardroom and began to meditate on the difference in value between the life of a machine and that of a human being. The guard played skat; the chief came along and told them to carry on while he had a chat with me. He seemed to find some difficulty in expressing himself. 'My dear chap,' he began, 'after what you showed him today . . . His Excellency seems to think you're a born scout . . . and . . . yes . . . His Excellency will let you off those three days' cells if . . . if you volunteer to train as a scout at once . . . ' 'Herr Captain,' I replied, 'I'll apply at once for a transfer to the Jagdstaffel School at Farmas.' I'll tell you about what happened there another time!"

Eight listeners pressed closely round the youth who had related his first unfortunate exploit without the slightest attempt at self-glorification. That was decent of him, they decided, and so, one after the other, they offered him brotherhood.

"Stop!" Kussin interrupted the solemn ceremony. "We other four will drink brotherhood with Hamann when he's got his first front flight behind him! We'll have to wait for that! There's a difference between exploits fifty kilometres behind the lines and those at the front! I wish the Englishmen would always make their appearance in the form of red and gold generals; I'd give them . . . !"

LIEUTENANT OLDEN AND BAUMANN

CHAPTER III

Six English balloons were up by Ypres. From their positions well behind their lines they were putting such a heavy artillery fire on to the German trenches that the defensive measures hitherto practised were unable to stay the devastating effect.

We are in the year 1918, when every feat must be rewarded. General Höppner has therefore announced that every balloon shot down shall count as two machines and carry a premium of 500 marks and a fortnight's leave as well. It means two steps up the ladder of fame, on the topmost rung of which gleams the *Pour le Mérite*.

But the six English balloons have cables by which they can communicate with the ground. In each basketwork car there is an observer who finds it an easy task to set the motor-winch in operation as soon as German machines approach. A few minutes later all six balloons are safely and snugly at rest.

Olden and his pilots were seized with ambition. Not so much on account of that distinguished order, and even a fortnight's leave can be a dubious blessing—fourteen days of life under something like peace conditions—only "something like," be it remembered—no, the most alluring bait was the 500 marks! But personal ambition was an even more potent motive. Money is not always the decisive factor!

Daily observations showed that the balloons always went up at 7.30 a.m. Field glasses revealed the fact that each balloon was encircled by a constant protective force of three English scouts, who were relieved at hourly intervals. Olden took off to attack the balloons with first one and then another of his pilots, but for tactical reasons he refused to launch his whole Staffel against them. He weighed every possibility carefully, because the lives of thousands of infantry comrades, exposed to the savage artillery fire in their trenches, were at stake.

The armoury master supplied the machine-guns with fresh ammunition. The first hundred rounds of every belt contained phosphorus bullets.

"Herr Lieutenant," said the armoury master, "I must give the new pilot strict warning in your presence. He must be careful with the phosphorus ammunition."

"I know, I know!" Hamann knew his instructions by heart.

"Well, and do you call the English careful, when we can prove they've been using the same bullets in their machine-guns for the last few months?" Baumann, the chief's first mechanic, muttered audibly.

Baumann's Bavarian temper was inflamed. This rage comes on a man suddenly, flames up—in the manner every Bavarian has inherited from his ancestors—and dies away or must be quenched in beer.

"Herr Lieutenant!" he buckled his chief carefully into his belt, "Herr Lieutenant, come back safe and sound! And give them a good dose of phosphorus. They're not polite enough to tell us beforehand what they've loaded their guns with."

Olden adjusted his goggles and nodded to his faithful watchdog. "Baumann, if I fetch those blimps down today, you can go off on leave."

The mechanic replied, but the roar of the engine swallowed up his words. The machines taxied across the aerodrome bathed in morning light, and a few minutes later Olden and Hamann were on their way to Ypres.

The tall, burly Baumann stood bareheaded, with his field-glasses glued to his eyes. Thus he followed every flight of the chief who was young enough to be his son. He never budged from his position until the brown Fokker with the streamers of leadership was "home" again.

"I say," he called out to the armoury master, "did you hear that? I can go on leave if he—Christ, what's he thinking about? God Almighty, am I going to leave the chief here alone?"

*   *   *

The tattered blanket of clouds floats about 1,000 metres up. Here and there fragments of it are forming balls, and through the gaps between these balls gleams the blue sky.

Hamann bends to look out of his machine. Below him there is a medley of trenches and thousands of the shell-holes which seem to have pierced the earth's skin. But all that sector of the front is quiet.

His chronometer shows 7.30 a.m.

The balloons are going up over yonder; they form a chain stretching southward from Ypres to Kemmel. One—two—three—four— But now the cloud blanket cuts off all visibility. Well, the other two will certainly not remain down below.

The new man is familiar with the state of things in the clouds and above the clouds. He knows how to read his view of the ground. He is at home in his machine and knows how to handle his two guns, the trigger-rings of which lie ready to the fore and middle fingers of his right hand—ready to pour forth destruction to the enemy and perhaps salvation to himself, at his bidding. He has received instruction in the various colours of the signal lights, and knows the significance of each. But what he does not know is the way in which the enemy must be attacked.

In his hours of solitude he had sufficient time to visualise a battle in the air. He often made the effort to enter into the spirit of an attack, but always found himself groping in a void. His leader and comrades have given him his "baptism" in the course of several front patrols. They have shown him the War—his trade which he has studied theoretically but can only learn to understand by practice.

He has acquired a dim notion of what to do and what not to do. But experience is only gained by a combination of theory and practice, and war does not permit the individual to waste much time on learning its art. That is why Olden made up his mind quickly to take the new man with him.

Now he is 800 metres up, following his chief's brown Fokker. A sense of security—the origin of which he cannot fathom—envelops his heart and brain. Perhaps it is love of life. Perhaps it is a feeling of comradeship or a love of flying. He cannot tell. He stares spellbound at every motion of his chief's arm. The excitement of the chase is in his blood. But the chief is calm, and Hamann remembers his warning: "So then, you'll keep above me and cover our retreat! If I manage to shoot one down, look out for the burst of flame, and don't fly into the burning sausage!"

They keep their engines well throttled down. Now they are flying just above the sea of clouds. Hamann is several hundred metres higher than his chief, and none of his movements escapes him.

The chief circles round the edge of a gap in the clouds. Hamann can see the never-ending line of trenches. There is a balloon on the left edge of the cloud-gap; its nationality marks—the red, white and blue rings—are plainly visible. The balloon and the ground lie in a deep, dark shadow.

Now, thinks Hamann, now! No, he does not really think anything at all. His engine is working regularly; his heart-beats are regular. Both engine and heart have one and the same rhythm. His glances are directed only towards the chief.

7.32 a.m. Three Sopwiths flit by close under the cloud-blanket. The relief machines are on their way to the trio. For a few seconds the balloon will be left unguarded.

The chief waggles his Fokker's wings three times. The signal for the attack.

Then he puts his machine down on to her nose—vanishes into the gap at lightning speed.

Hamann can scarcely follow the next events with his eyes, But he has learnt to fly—he has learnt to fly well. He puts his machine on to her nose and hurtles after the chief. His wings whistle. A nose-dive of 400 metres in a matter of a few seconds.

They have fallen through the hole in the clouds. The sudden change from the dazzling glare of white-hot sunlight to the deepest, gloomiest shadows deprive the two pilots of their vision for the moment. Hamann pulls his machine up level instinctively, lest this mad, headlong dive should send him crashing into the chief's Fokker. But his eyes still find difficulty in accustoming themselves to this light.

Suddenly he sees something burning far below him. A huge tongue of flame sweeps earthward; a blazing balloon goes down to the depths. Far behind it is the chief's machine. Follow the chief!

Suddenly the air is full of English scouts.

The second balloon is hauled down by the motor-winch. It is only 50 metres above the ground. The chief swoops down like a hawk. A flame—and the balloon is finished.

The fire of the Archies forces Olden to climb in a steeply banked turn and head for the German trenches.

Eight Sopwiths chase off after the chief, but they cannot catch him. His machine is the faster. They pay no attention to Hamann, who is 700 metres higher. Below him lies the English aerodrome of Poperinghe. Thirty-three machines rise up from it like a swarm of bees.

Hamann sees thirty-three machines—they are looking for him and will find him. What were his orders? "Cover the retreat!"

The other balloons are hauled down. The third is safely on the ground, and by their plate-shaped steel helmets the crowd of soldiers round it would seem to be Americans.

Three batteries are firing. They are protecting the balloon on the ground.

The point on the horizon has vanished. The white cloudlets of the Archies still mark its way home. Perhaps the chief is already across; perhaps he has landed and is in the mess.

So now Hamann is alone. Alone against thirty-three machines and an uncountable number of Archies. Alone!

He puts his machine down on to her nose and dives until he is almost at the level of the trees.

How those Americans run! The broad envelope of the inflated sausage lies before him.

A curt tack-tack of his machine-guns! Phosphorus bullets! And for the third time he sees flames—livid white flames! . . .

"Look out for the burst of flame, and don't fly into the burning sausage!" Was that just a memory or Olden's voice again?

He flits across the trenches at barely 20 metres' height. From below Americans, Englishmen, Frenchmen—every man who can put a rifle to his shoulder—fires at him; from above the machine-guns of the enemy Archies hail down on him, with bright shrapnels coming in between the bullets.

The English are tenacious. They chase the German far beyond the trenches and far beyond his aerodrome, in the direction of Brussels. But at last the German Archies make their presence felt. The Fokker has the speed of the Sopwiths, but the English take their revenge. They send a few German mechanics scuttling to cover and shoot up a petrol depot. Then they go into a turn and fly off westwards.

Hamann lands. His limbs are somewhat stiff.

The mechanics show him the bullet-holes in his wings.

He nods his head—yes, yes.

He stares at his machine—first attentively and then absentmindedly. He would like to do something nice to it—a man to a machine—but he does not know what to do. But perhaps this is merely a sudden silly attack of weakness.

That was the first front flight in which he took a hand in a scrap. Really it was all quite different from what he imagined it would be. Nice? Or not nice? Was it a good show? He thought he had better have a wash before deciding and pour cold water over his head—lots of cold water!

He found them all seated in the mess.

"Come here!" shouted the chief above the general din. "You don't need to report it; the front line trenches have rung up to tell us!"

Hamann had to shake many hands.

"Look here," said the chief, "that's our third balloon! You can say 'thou'* to me now—if you like!"

---

* It is naturally impossible to translate the second person singular, which is only used between intimates in continental languages, into English.
—Translator's note

PILOT OF JAGDSTAFFEL 356

Chapter IV

The Staffel has been patrolling the front for the last twenty minutes. The chief heads the V formation; the other ten machines follow in open order. The last machine, which flies high above the rest, contains the look-out man. His keen eyes scan the sky before and behind him, to right and left, for a sign of the enemy. He is the pet objective of all pugnacious enemy airmen. The pilots speak of him as the "hare."

All machine-guns have fresh ammunition supplies; the tanks under the seats are well filled.

In the far distance, somewhere about 2,500 metres above Dickebusch Lake, four blue German naval Fokkers are engaged with eight Sopwiths.

The brown Staffel hurries on, for the blue Fokkers are going round and round each other in steeply-banked turns. A bad sign. They emit short bursts every now and then. They whirl round one another, towards one another, grimly seeking an opportune moment to get the enemy in their sights, for the only certain range is something under 30 metres.

One Sopwith flies above the fray, quietly waiting its chance. Already they can recognise the long fluttering streamers; it is Captain Bishop, the English master-scout.

Now he swoops—a blue Fokker rears up wildly and hurtles in a blaze to the depths, leaving a long trail of smoke behind it.

The chief and his Staffel are now within range. The closed formation opens out.

The chief and Bishop charge at one another.

The tack-tack-tack of machine-guns rings sharply in the ears.

All the machines are going into turns and tail-chasing. The sky is wide, but here are twenty machines huddled together at the closest quarters. Their tanks are still full; men and machine-guns seem welded into units. Machine rages against machine—but then they calculate their chances coolly and deliberately. Where is the weak spot exposed by the enemy? It is a horrible game of cat and mouse!

Steffen roars, but cannot hear his own voice. All sensations and ears are deafened by the whirr of the propeller.

There is a Sopwith above him; he knows its pilot is now turning his machine-gun on him. He pulls his Fokker up. For a few seconds the phosphorus lines cut their way to the Sopwith above.

A tongue of flame—Steffen has hit the enemy's petrol tank. The burning liquid trickles out.

The blazing Sopwith reels; the flames continue to devour it. For a moment Steffen has a vision of a mask-like face. The other pilot tears his glasses off.

"Jump for it!" Steffen screams to him. "Jump with your parachute!"

He goes into a wide turn. The English machine is glowing, but it can still fly. It follows Steffen with a crazy accuracy. Steffen thinks he can hear the crackle of the flames and the hiss of melting metal. The man inside it must be on fire! Why doesn't he pull his safety belt off?

"Parachute!"

Steffen roars—but the horror follows him. Is the Englishman trying to ram him with his last strength?

THREE PILOTS OF
JAGDSTAFFEL 356

HAMANN AT THE
AGE OF 17.

HAMANN IN 1918,
AFTER THE WAR.

Steffen goes into a turn—the Englishman follows—a blazing, smoking pillar of fire. Steffen does not hear the thud of the machine-gun bullets in his Fokker. Behind him still hurtles the Englishman in raging pursuit—nearer—nearer comes the mad thing. To think that a burning machine can fly so long! How much longer?

A sharp, shrill crack—the Sopwith has burst into fragments. Steffen sees bits of it hurtling to the depths. He cannot, however, see any sign of a human being.

Bishop and the chief are still circling round one another.

As the Englishman flits by, he fires at a brown Fokker. The wings catch fire at once; the machine goes down in flames. It hits the surface of Dickebusch Lake and promptly sinks into it.

A black pillar of smoke hovers over the scene of its crash for a long time.

The chief keeps up a furious fire on Bishop. He shoots away all his ammunition. No use. The Englishman is out of range.

The cramped mass breaks up. Machines disengage. The Sopwiths flock together. The blue and brown Fokkers form a squadron.

They fly home.

One brown Fokker is missing.

A Fokker D.VII

Chapter V

On the afternoon of the same day the paymaster came to see the chief.

"The commissariat depot has refused to give you the quantity of meat you applied for, sir."

"Indeed? Refused, have they?" There was a vague look in the chief's eyes which was seldom seen there. When it appeared, it boded ill for someone. "So the base-wallahs refuse, do they? The base-wallahs, eh? Baumann, go into the mess and say I shan't be able to dine with the gentlemen!"

Olden and his paymaster went into the town by car; they made straight for the well-filled flesh-pots of the commissariat officers.

What transpired there has never been quite explained. The chief said nothing about it; the captain at the base would only express himself in writing, and the paymaster shook his head. But he, at least, had something to report.

After the exchange of a few introductory remarks in a voice from which all efforts at courtesy soon died out, the chief suddenly smote the table in a fit of rage and was heard to scream through the barrack-room window: "Herr Captain, my men work day and night; you will understand that they must also have something to eat!" The reservist captain, a man in the fifties, agreed, but protested his inability to do anything more.

He was, however, incapable of holding his own against Bavarian profanity, and was likewise somewhat cowed by the *Pour le Mérite* worn by the lieutenant of some twenty-six years, for as a celebrity the latter was a person to be feared. But the chief's success was only a negative one, for the captain yielded him up no further supplies.

But meanwhile the paymaster scrounged a newly-slaughtered swine, which he loaded up into the car with the chief's assistance.

The chief stood a cask of beer that evening for the men's canteen, and for the next few days the meat rations and consequently the general tone were satisfactory once more.

But the captain at the base drew up a letter of complaint which gave sufficient bureaucratic employment in the offices of various superior authorities.

CHAPTER VI

For some days past a Belgian one-seater had been keeping all the Flanders Staffels busy. He shot down German balloons with a cold-blooded accuracy that could almost be termed impudence, so that the Staffel-leaders held a conference to discuss measures to deal with him.

Every other day the same events took place with the regularity of clockwork. At 7 a.m. a German balloon went up. At 7.25 a.m. white shrapnel cloudlets in the sky signalled the approach of the Belgian machine. At 7.30 a.m. the balloon crew received the telegraphic message: "Enemy aircraft! Jump!" Three minutes, at the latest, after they had jumped, the balloon went down in flames.

They changed the balloon's position—in vain! All the efforts of the Fokkers proved unavailing, all bullets seemed to rebound from the Belgian. Was there in this sober modern war a charm for invulnerability? Was there a miracle? Was there a magic circle round the swift machine? The wildest rumours were current—some new fantastic invention. . . .

A trio took off. Olden, Mierdl and Strantz. No success.

"I got him in my sights at twenty metres, and he flew between the phosphorus lines like a fly passing through cigarette smoke!" Strantz was quite upset.

A Belgian solved the mystery. The machine was a new type, with an armoured fuselage. It had stood the test splendidly and was to be copied in large quantities.

Olden read this report over and over again in silence. He thought of the machines flown by his Staffel. There had been a shortage of materials for some time; nickel brass and bronze were no longer to be had; there was nothing but iron. The word "substitute" figured larger in vocabularies from day to day. The mechanics mended and repaired with the skill of magicians; they worked carefully and found all sorts of makeshifts. Every one of them had earned the *Pour le Mérite.*

So the fellow had an armoured machine. His name was Roeppen. He was a second-lieutenant, a Fleming by birth and pride of Belgian aviation.

But an armour-plated Fokker was not a machine to be turned out overnight.

One day Roeppen put the finishing touch to his magic work. He shot down the training balloon belonging to the Artillery Observers' School at Valenciennes. That meant a long flight behind the lines.

The major who was O.C. Balloons decided to take his own measures. He planned to send up a balloon filled with explosives; its crew was to be two straw dummies dressed up in officers' coats and caps. The bullets from the Belgian's machine-guns would naturally explode the dynamite, and then the huge pieces of iron in the car would fly out and destroy his machine. The preparations for this low trick took three days.

Olden and the leader of the neighbouring Staffel heard of it in time. All their pilots were of one opinion: "We'd rather let him shoot us all down than wage that sort of war. We'll fight, but we're not going to treat our opponent like a mad dog!"

"Don't talk so much! Do something!" screamed the balloon major, "You're making yourselves ridiculous to the whole world! If you can't bring that Belgian down in the next forty-eight hours, I'll carry out my plan. I'll report you for obstructing me in my operations of war!"

Olden turned his back on the enraged major. He had a long and intensive conference with the observation officers. None of them had received further orders to go up since Roeppen had started to make a nuisance of himself, and there were times when no one volunteered for the job.

"I'll come along with my Staffel tomorrow. The naval crowd will try to hold the lad up. Be ready to jump for it any moment!"

The youthful sergeant nodded. "I can't do more than wish yourself and myself the best of luck. This blighter—all the same one can't help admiring him!"

"So Hals und Beinbruch, comrade!"

The next morning showed a real Flanders sky. There was nothing to be seen above 900 metres, but there was good ground visibility below that height.

The decoy balloon went up near Rosclare. Five blue naval Fokkers circled round it; five others were ready to take off from the emergency landing-ground.

The brown Fokkers flown by Olden, Baum, Kussin, Strantz, Rom and Mierdl circled above them in wide sweeps; the other machines of the Staffel patrolled the outer area in open order.

Archie's cloudlets marked the Belgian's path. Olden flew off to give him a friendly welcome and fired down into the uncovered pilot's seat.

The surprised Roeppen went into a right-hand turn. Strantz cut across it. He had a feeling that the Belgian was laughing at him. The blood rushed to his head.

"Oh, damn the blighter!"

Strantz shoots. The chief shoots. The Belgian shoots. The balloon is hauled down hastily.

The magic machine is surrounded by foes above and below it, to right and left of it.

Roeppen puts up a desperate resistance. A spider's web of tracers has been spun round his machine.

Roeppen tries to make the English lines, but the ring of brown Fokkers around him grows ever narrower.

Suddenly the Belgian's bursts cease.

The former hussar lieutenant Baum is such a little fellow that his mechanic had to put a block 20 centimetres thick on the rudder bar before he could reach it with his feet. Little Baum forces his Fokker down in steep spirals; he stares down at Roeppen. The redoubtable foeman's guns have jammed; they have let him down!

Roeppen is a skilled pilot and up to all tricks of his trade. He forces his machine down lower and lower in search of a gap which will enable him to make a dive lor the English lines. But he promptly receives a burst in his cockpit.

The ring of brown Fokkers is like a wall. Only the supreme skill of the pilots averts a collision. And now they have forced Roeppen down to the level of the houses.

At last he gives up. He lands in a turnip field near the Roulers-Tourhout road with a broken propeller. He jumps out desperately; his face is coated with grey patches from the powder smoke. He opens an armour plate of his machine, which he means to set on fire with a shot from his Verey Pistol.

But Mierdl has already landed close beside him. He fires a warning, threatening burst over Roeppen's head.

The Belgian surrenders in despair.

The Germans examine with amazed eyes the magic machine which has fallen into their hands intact and undamaged. The chief invites Roeppen to go along with him to the aerodrome in his car. Ten Germans sit down at table to breakfast with a Belgian, who receives the attentions of an honoured guest. The French they learnt at school must serve them to exchange flying yarns with their guest —for, first and foremost, they are all airmen. A comradely sense of tact eases the situation until the Intelligence Officer arrives from H.Q. to remind them that Lieutenant Roeppen is a prisoner of war.

Victor and Vanquished: the little Fokker and
the huge English fighter it forced down

CHAPTER VII

The Staffel's encounter with Captain Bishop claimed a victim.
A brown Fokker went down in flames to Dickebusch Lake.

No one can choose his own death-bed, and least of all the soldier. This time there was no chaplain, no music, and no wreaths; there was not even a coffin.

Eleven took off, and ten landed. Did Schlosske feel his number was up when he started that day? Certainly not. No one has such presentiments. Or, at least, no one admits them. One climbs into one's machine, flies, fires and leaves the rest to what some call "Chance," others "Destiny" and yet others "God."

But Schlosske's chair in the mess was empty. Once again someone packed up personal belongings and despatched them to the dead man's home. This time, however, no photograph of a newly-turned grave-mound could be included; never will the family be able to visit this land and search the many rows of wooden crosses for the name of "Herbert Schlosske." There are so many, unending rows of these wooden crosses standing erect today—tomorrow, perhaps, they will be mown down by a shell or an airman's bomb.

Lieutenant Olden applied for a new man.

To put it in a nutshell, he wanted a daring pilot and a cold-blooded hunter. The art of aerial warfare is to attack a machine as though it were a wild beast and then use the machine-guns with deadly marksmanship in the brief space of a second. Each man has his own special tactics; one aims at the petrol tank, another fires from above at the unprotected cockpit, while a third makes the engine his mark. The fighting pilot is thrown absolutely on his own resources. He, and he alone, has the chances.

The enemy's lines receive the Staffel with anti-aircraft fire.

If there are no enemy aircraft in sight, the idle pilots may perhaps have a game of "shrapnels," which is played in the following fashion. If the gunners on the ground below are placing their shells just a little too far to the left, the whole Staffel goes into a left-hand turn in close order and flies through the white cloudlets formed by the shell-bursts. If, on the other hand, the enemy's range is too far to the right, the Staffel goes into an elegant right-hand turn and flies through the white cloudlets. If, however, the bark of the shrapnels comes unpleasantly nearer, then the game has to stop.

When the formation reaches the aerial battlefield, the pilots must attack their opponents, no matter whether they are one to one, one to three, one to four or one to some higher figure. The individual must not, however, lose his general survey of the situation; he must always keep one eye on his leader and be ready to come to the aid of a comrade in extreme danger. If he wins a victory over an enemy machine which comes down on the German side of the lines, his victim's number-plate, propeller, mascot, etc., become his trophies. If he is shot down himself, his last hope of salvation lies in the parachute buckled round him. Its folds serve him as a cushion while he is flying.

Great presence of mind is needed by the pilot who makes use of this way of escape. When he is absolutely certain that his machine has been shot down and will crash, he must unbuckle the safety belt which enables him to go safely into nose-dives or steeply banked turns, and jump overboard. He must then count on the probability

A Farman Biplane shot down in flames

of coming down on unknown territory, on ground torn up by shells, on tree stumps, ruins of shelled houses, marshes or the enemy's lines.

The new man must be equal to all these demands which will be made upon him.

The D.7 Fokker was thoroughly overhauled, and one morning its occupant arrived. He came to the Staffel as a tall, thin horseman with a slight stoop, with blue eyes and a gleaming eye-glass, with thin fair hair, carefully combed back, that covered a small, angular head. He was Prince Johann Georg, a scion of one of the smaller German princely houses.

"Good Lord, a prince!" thought the comrades.

It is true that a prince comes into the world in just the same way as other mortals, but one is easily inclined to attribute particular qualities to such personalities. How would he fit in? Would he observe the comradeship as faithfully as those who received him into their midst? Princely privileges could not be respected in the Staffel, and there were no lackeys to attend on him.

The chief was in somewhat of a dilemma. He had to give the newcomer the usual few words of greeting. "Your Highness," he began, "our motto is 'Comrades in the air and comrades on the ground'; we are all one family" He paused—what a difficult job it is to make a speech! "Your Highness, we are happy—"

The object of his oration stood before him in a careless and slightly disdainful attitude. "Oh, please, drop all these ceremonies," he said with a laugh. "They're all rot!" He turned a gleaming eye-glass on to pilot after pilot. "My name is Johann Georg, and we'll leave the 'Highness' for home consumption. What are all your names?"

Audible sighs of relief. Really quite a nice fellow, so it seemed, although a bit familiar. Well, one could get used to the eye-glass in time!

He was twenty-one years old and a member of the *garde du corps*; he ate, slept, bathed, rode and flew with his eye-glass, but the thin, small, birdlike head was always full of new witticisms and good stories. Behind all these externals there was a good-natured, amiable boyish mentality, innocent enough to admit that what he liked best in life was chocolate pudding with vanilla sauce.

His ten comrades gave him the usual three days' instruction in the practical details of aerial warfare which all newcomers received.

It so happened at that time that the Staffel had a problem to solve. Their ample experiences of the previous week had demonstrated that Sopwith pilots found considerable difficulty in going into right-hand turns, probably on account of the opposing pull of the rotary engine. Rom, who was a true German in his thoroughness, put forward the theory that the left-hand turn must come naturally easier to anyone, because the heart is on the left-hand side. He got his mechanics to experiment on motor-cycles and found, in fact, that they all showed a better balance when turning to the left. So the brown Fokkers practised the fastest and most steeply banked right-hand turns until they were perfect in them.

Then Olden, Rom, Hamann and Strantz took the prince in their midst to test the effect of the Ypres Archies on the new man.

"Prince," said the chief, "when we tumble into a scrap—and you seldom know beforehand when one's coming along—dive down three hundred metres and look on! If any machine attacks you, go into a steeply banked right-hand turn at once, you understand!"

"Man alive, I'm not going to bolt," replied the prince. "I'll stop with you and carry on!"

They took off for the front and flew comfortably through the air warmed by the noontide sun. The prince was safely tucked away between the four of them, and watched every movement they made with due attention.

Suddenly they found themselves underneath seven Sopwiths,

which seemed to have dropped out of the clouds. The Englishmen must have seen the black Maltese cross on the wings of the German machines and the leader's streamers clearly enough in that bright light, for they calculated their dives to an inch when they came down on the brown Fokkers.

The Germans promptly went into a steeply banked right-hand turn.

"Come on, Prince, turn!" roared Strantz. He knew his voice could not even penetrate ten metres, but he hoped his wish would inspire the new man.

The chief is entangled in a fight with two opponents; the machine-guns are pounding away. A moment ago the machines were to right and left of him—now they are above and below him—it is a battle fought out in all dimensions. Nevertheless he finds time to cast a glance in the direction of the prince, who had received the instructions, given to all new men, that he must be only a spectator of his first fight.

An Englishman dives on Johann Georg, whose machine is seen to reel. "Has that unexpected attack made him lose his head?" wonders Strantz.

The Archies howl up from the ground; at 3,000 metres up seven Englishmen are flying round four Germans.

All of a sudden the prince realises the purpose of it all and the significance of the scouting pilot. He pulls his stick across. His fore and middle fingers put his machine-guns in action. The Sop with is within thirty metres of him—there go the bullets—tack—tack—tack!

Hamann is defending himself against three machines. He fires, whirls past one of them, goes into a right-hand turn, comes back, pulls his stick up—emits streams of phosphorus into a cockpit! How those Sopwiths lose height with every right-hand turn! Good enough! Carry on with the right-hand turns—like a merry-go-round!

An Englishman disengages himself from Strantz, but returns—is he trying to ram the prince after firing away all his ammunition? The two machines whizz close by one another—the wings almost seem to bend up with the crazy pace!

Tack—tack—the prince's machine-guns hammer out curtly and drily.

The Sopwith is hit!

A kick at the rudder-bar! The prince hurtles close past the Englishman. He sees the pilot is wounded—his head droops—his helmet and face are covered with blood.

The prince ceases fire; he knows the chivalrous customs of the scouting pilot. In wide turns he follows the reeling machine, which makes a last desperate effort to reach the English lines.

Then suddenly all six Englishmen break off the fight and follow their comrade. Who is he that they should take such care of him? Perhaps another new man?

Four German Fokkers form up for the homeward flight.

As soon as the prince lands, he goes up to the chief and stands at attention before him. He puts his hand up to his helmet and his eye-glass gleams as he announces: "Beg to report my first victory, Sopwith, blue and yellow colours, Ypres sector, 3,200 metres' height, time 11.40 a.m., opponent wounded."

Hamann is the first to congratulate the prince. He is now a veteran war pilot and expresses himself benevolently concerning the remarkable luck the other has experienced in shooting down an opponent on his first front patrol. Hamann and the prince—the one is seventeen, the other twenty-one!

Schulz, the locksmith, stands at the door of the mess in his blue overalls and tries to attract the chief's tatention. Olden rises and goes to him.

"Well, what's up?" he enquires in the Bavarian dialect.

Schulz, a volunteer of forty-three years, gives vent to a couple of hard gulps and then says: "Herr Lieutenant, I only wanted to report—I would like to—"

"Yes—?" says the chief. He pushes the man out and closes the door behind him.

"My son is dead," says the mechanic in quick, low tones.

"Would you like to have leave and go home to your wife, Schulz?"

"No, no, that's no good. But—" Schulz breaks off and wipes his oil-smeared face with his hand. "He was only twenty—and a volunteer, too. His regiment was last heard of on the Isonzo. I know it. I know how he died too. Buried alive—I've got definite news— buried alive. Herr Lieutenant, I've seen what they look like in hospital when they've been buried alive!"

Olden tries to say something, but Schulz continues. He murmurs abrupt broken sentences. He has to go on saying something. All his comrades take their troubles to the chief. He is such a good listener—and that is all they want.

"Can you tell me, sir—"

The chief shakes the man's arm. "Schulz, perhaps he hasn't been buried alive. Perhaps he is in hospital. Perhaps he got a clean bullet through the head—"

"No, Herr Lieutenant, I know—I feel it—"

Schulz's voice chokes. He breaks off suddenly, assumes an attitude of attention and says in completely changed accents: "Thank you, Herr Lieutenant. I only wanted to report it to you, sir."

The chief takes the man's hand. "Schulz, if you would like to go home, perhaps. You can have a week—"

"No thanks, Herr Lieutenant!" The man turns and goes.

Olden does not know the younger Schulz—the twenty-year-old volunteer who was buried alive on the Isonzo, but he has known Schulz, the Landsturm man, for the last two years. He knows every man in his Staffel and sundry other good comrades besides. Many

Above: ROM'S FATAL CRASH; *below:* ROM'S FURNERAL

of them have died as heroes, yes, many have died heroic deaths, but new men always come to take their places!

"Got to do some work!" thinks the chief, and then, all of a sudden, he feels the responsibility for nearly a hundred souls resting heavily on his shoulders. A heavy burden! And then, all at once, it occurs to him that he is only twenty-six years old.

CHAPTER VIII

Hamann and Kussin are off to Brussels. It is their turn to have a few hours off to amuse themselves. Dancing halls, wine restaurants and theatres are at their disposal.

Over the doors of the dancing halls there were notice-boards which drew their attention in French and German to the fact that they were reserved "For Officers only." They knew that life in such places was generally rather dull and bourgeois. The officers of the base took their meals in them; they drank a lot and played innumerable hands of cards. Distinctions of rank were strictly observed, so that it was obvious the people there would have little sympathy for all the good and bad customs of the front which clung to them.

It is easy to understand that Kussin and Hamann executed all their commissions as quickly as possible, because everyone who took such leave had to buy all sorts of things for his comrades. Rom was extravagant in his use of soap, Mierdl smoked a special brand of cigarettes and was keen on getting hold of the latest dance tunes, Steffen used incredible quantities of note-paper and Olden was always needing new socks. So they visited the shops most conscientiously, made their choice slowly, examined the qualities of everything carefully and made their purchases.

Then at last they were ready to let the fair town of Brussels and its inhabitants give them the pleasures they might expect. But the population seemed to consist mainly of German soldiers; the civilians led such retired lives that they were hardly noticeable as part of the street scene.

"We don't want to go in the same old holes where I'm not supposed to go as an N.C.O., or where I have to march about between the tables as if I was on parade," said Kussin.

It was a very warm spring day; the corpulent Kussin wiped his brow with his new silk handkerchief. They stood before the cathedral; the perfume of incense floated through the open doors; candles and flowers shone in the semi-darkness of the interior. They stood there gazing for a long time, but did not dare to enter. There seemed to be something mysterious—almost awe-inspiring—in the way those solid ancient walls looked down century after century on the troubles of the day. Almost every hour of their days at the front, they were in close contact with the life beyond the grave, and so it was incomprehensible to them that stones piled up by mortal hands should live longer than they themselves. They sensed only the incense, the flowers and the candles, and all the desires of their youthful dreams clamoured for fulfilment.

"Come along!" said Kussin. They passed on quickly—aimlessly, yet with a definite goal before them. They were both still very young, and so they did not give utterance to their thoughts and hopes—of meeting a woman. They did not want the women whom the solicitous military authorities kept at their disposal in certain quarters; they were seeking the woman whose tender image was a vision in both their inexperienced hearts.

Narrow winding streets opened up before them—a strange town which they had never seen before. And then they saw a signboard: Café Leonidas.

They both halted. School memories. "Leonidas? One of those old Greeks! Battle of Thermopylæ!" With these words Kussin demonstrated that his parents had paid his school fees to some good purpose.

"That was the man who died with his three hundred Spartans!" Hamann beamed at the thought of his knowledge. "Well, let's go in!"

They were welcomed by a strip of red coconut matting, which ran in a straight line before them, right to the end of the room. Its gay colour looked promising, but it represented the "No Man's Land."

In the first room there was a buffet, which said nothing definite. In the second and larger room there was a notice on the left of the matting which said: "For Soldiers Only." N.C.O.s, paymasters and petty officers from the ships in Flanders waters sat in this portion. To the right of the matting there was a notice which proclaimed: "For Civilians Only," and there sat the obedient civilians.

The two pilots stood on their neutral ground and stared to the right. They saw harmless women of the bourgeoisie, young girls, older girls—more or less chic—all eating ices, as was fit and proper on this warm May day.

The conversation on the male side of the apartment was carried on in low, quiet tones; the conversation on the female side was almost a series of whispers.

Hamann gave his friend a nudge. "I say, we've got to sit down!"

Kussin craned his head forward and listened. "The matting goes on to another room!" he whispered excitedly.

Yes, the red strip of coconut matting actually vanished behind a velvet curtain. Laughs resounded from the other side. Instruments were being tuned up there. The couple crept forward on tiptoe in the direction of these sounds.

The third room of the Cafe Leonidas was its sensation; to the strains of a well-meaning string band German soldiers and Belgian ladies were dancing on a floor as smooth as a mirror.

Hamann let the curtain fall again. The two stared at one another in pallid silence. Neither could find words to comment on this great revelation They could dance and drink wine with girls! With really nice young girls—just like at home!

"Is my hair parted straight?" Kussin fanned himself with his new silk handkerchief. Hamann stared at his hands, which still bore unmistakable traces of oil. "My boy, my boy!" But one thing seemed certain, and that was the fact that they must first find seats on German territory.

They ordered wine and listened to the strains of "The Beautiful Blue Danube."

"Bah!" said Kussin, and lit a cigarette with much display. "Those little girls will be only too pleased if we ask them!"

"Don't shout so! Well, then see how much French you can talk!" Hamann had not quite lost his shyness.

"Mademoiselle, voulez-vous dancer avec moi?" Then, after a period of doubt: "That's right, isn't it?"

"I don't know," replied Hamann, staring absent-mindedly across the red dividing line of coconut matting into the darkest corner of the room.

There sat four flappers, who laughed incessantly, told each other stories incessantly and yet found time to spoon up their ices in a nice, well-bred way. The Café Leonidas was the only one where ices could be obtained, which was a reason why it received such good patronage from the ladies.

"I say, it's just like being at home," observed Hamann. "I took my coaching at Schmidt's cake-shop, until my father spotted the trick!"

"Oh, go on, screw up your courage!" Kussin pulled his tunic down and made preparations to cross the matting.

"You mustn't do that!" protested the horrified Hamann. The waves of the beautiful blue Danube had reached the sea. The music ceased; the velvet curtain parted. A very elegant lady threw a few joyous words back over her shoulder into the dancehall and then walked towards the door, swiftly but with a very erect and haughty bearing. The waiter held the door open for her, and his "Bon soir, madame!" sounded like a tribute of homage.

Kussin and Hamann stared after her. She was—yes, she was the vision of their dreams—the woman of their lives.

They drank and smoked a lot. They did not speak much, but their thoughts were at work all the time. They praised the chance that brought them to the Café Leonidas. But how to "conquer" her? They were men now, but in thirty hours their leave would be over.

"Come on, we'll ask those kids over there," said Kussin suddenly.

He extracted a visiting card from his pocket-book with a grandiloquent gesture and wrote on it: "Mademoiselles, will you permit us to dance with you?"

The waiter took the card across. Hamann could not stop blush after blush surging across his face. Kussin puffed at his cigarette.

The laughter at the flappers' table died down. The waiter smiled discreetly.

The two youths dared not look up. They heard coins clink on the marble-topped table, and the sound of chairs being pushed back. The four maidens rose, collected their gloves and bags and left the café. Their refusals and embarrassment were plainly written on their faces, but they did not vouchsafe a single glance to the German side of the room.

That moment was a harder one for Kussin and Hamann than any in which they had faced the sharpest burst from an enemy machine-gun. They could hold their own in the fiercest fight in the air, but they were ignorant of the way in which to set about the conquest of a woman.

A genial but malicious laugh resounded from a neighbouring table.

"You're a couple of silly kids!" a naval petty officer called across to them, and his companions, who had likewise watched the course of the incident, joined in the laughter. Well-meaning but uncouth words of jest rose from their lips. Kussin and Hamann sat overwhelmed by their blushes.

"Of course you can strike up an acquaintance here," said another petty officer with kindly intent. "But there's nothing doing with that smart piece of work who went out just now. She lives on nothing but ice, it seems!"

"Oh, indeed!" said Kussin, who had regained his "man of the world" air. He buckled his belt, paid and whistled loudly as he marched towards the door. Hamann tossed his cap into the air and caught it as he followed him.

CHAPTER IX

All the maps issued by the General Staff to the various formations were redrawn to incorporate the very latest information. Even the most insignificant advance of German forces or alteration in the line of trenches was carefully marked on them. Five hundred metres won here—three hundred lost there. And so it had gone on day by day for months—trench warfare!

Every day four brown Fokkers flew the front patrols allotted to them, seeking enemy airmen, noting alterations in the infantry positions and winding their way through the shrapnel cloudlets.

It was June, 1918. French Breguet two-seaters crossed the German lines frequently and flew far into the hinterland, where they dropped bundles of leaflets, with texts such as: "Soldiers, don't let them slave-drive you any longer! Your wives are starving at home! The Pope wants peace! Stop the War!"

Fighting machines of the Breguet type were seldom seen in this Flanders sector. The French machines flew chiefly along the line of trenches to protect their own positions, leaving the hunting work to the English and American scouts.

Four enemy aircraft appeared on the horizon. Steffen, who was acting as "hare," signalled their rapid approach with a red light, so that Kussin, Baum and Mierdl could know that four French ob-

Above: CAPTAIN STRATS' MACHINE
Below: CAPTAIN STRATS WITH THE INTELLIGENCE OFFICERS

servers were already training their machine-guns on them.

Baum dives down in a furious onslaught on the machine on the extreme left. "I must get one more, and then the chief can put me in for the first-class Iron Cross!" he said only this morning.

They all knew his sad history. His sister was married at the beginning of the War, but her husband fell in Belgium in August, 1914. She succumbed to an attack of melancholia and had to go to a mental home. Baum, who was a hussar officer, put in for a transfer to a Jagdstaffel.

"I must shoot them down!" he said. "I want to shoot them down, shoot down as many as I can, because they have ruined the happiness of my family!" He studied aeronautical science, devised plans for attacks on the enemy; with the help of his keen intellect, he worked night and day. The comrades who often envied him his great store of knowledge warned him in vain. They tried to show him how senseless it was to make all the enemy responsible for one man's work. In vain.

Kussin, the deputy-leader of today's patrol, sees that the quivering lines of phosphorus from Baum's machine have missed the Breguet. Then he sees his friend pull his machine up again and renew his attack on the foeman.

Steffen and Mierdl have become inattentive fighters. They fire their bursts, but turn back again and again towards Baum, whose nerves are obviously on edge. How many hours was he reading yesterday? He is doing one silly thing after another today!

The French machines stand out black against the red sky of evening. White balls of cloud mark the path of the English Archies.

The Breguets fire. Baum replies, and then his Fokker rears up steeply and suddenly. His engine is hit.

The German machine heels over. The safety belt has been shot through. It gives way; Baum falls out and hurtles downward like a stone.

The French scatter. They do not want to be rammed by the pilotless machine, which flies on for another fifty metres. Then its nose goes down, and it plunges into the depths.

Three comrades watch with beating hearts. The weight of the body hanging on the cord connecting the parachute with the machine causes it to break, and the parachute opens with a loud crack. Baum sways gently as he floats down, but it will be necessary for the wind to drift him away; otherwise he will go down into his burning Fokker or into the enemy's lines.

Kussin charges between the Frenchmen, with raging hatred in his heart; he pulls his machine round to this side and that, firing all the time, Mierdl joins the others; the antiquated Fokkers drive the new fast Breguets before them like hares. They see the observers working their machine-guns—and then the Frenchmen make for their own lines to escape the berserk Germans.

Steffen flies in wide circles round the sinking Baum. The latter seems to be unconscious, for he makes no movement. His clothing is torn and stained with blood. The evening breeze drifts him far across the lines, in the direction of Poperinghe aerodrome.

Heedless of the Archies and the machine-guns which join in from the ground, Kussin, Mierdl and Steffen follow him. Mierdl fires a red signal-light: "Help!"

Baum does not move. He hangs motionless in his belt. He glides gently down to a meadow. The ample folds of the parachute flop softly on to him.

The three German machines are flying only ten metres above the ground. Once more they fire a red signal light to entice the soldiers out of their cover.

At last some Americans come along. Neither side exchanges a shot. The Germans see Baum released from his parachute and carried away. He is still unconscious; blood wells up from under his helmet and runs down his face in a continuous flow. Then the three

Above: AN ENGLISH MACHINE SHOT DOWN IN FLAMES.
Below: THE WRECKAGE OF A GERMAN MACHINE SHOT DOWN
IN THE AIR BATTLE OF BRUGES. THE CART SEEN IN THE
BACKGROUND WAS PROPELLED A DISTANCE OF 15 METRES
BY THE AIR PRESSURE WHILE THE MACHINE BURIED ITSELF
3 METRES DEEP IN THE GROUND.

turn and fly home. The white parachute lies forsaken in the meadows.

Four weeks later a postcard from a hospital for prisoners of war was forwarded by the Geneva Red Cross. Baum wrote briefly that he was doing well so far.

That postcard was the last sign of life he gave. Afterwards he vanished. All possible post-war researches in London, Paris and elsewhere yielded no results. The casualty lists could only note the fate of the hussar lieutenant Baum as "Missing."

CHAPTER X

A telephone message: enemy bombing squadron sighted, flying in the direction of Bruges.

Two cars, which were always at hand, convey ten pilots across the aerodrome to the machines which lie ready to take off. They fly westwards, in the direction of Bruges.

Height: 1,200 metres. They fly in echelon, as usual. Nine pairs of eyes are fixed, as if spellbound, on the chief, who leads and flies lowest.

The chief waves his right arm. They all go into a right-hand turn automatically. They have been flying for half an hour now. They can see nothing; they can only hear. They hear the whirr of the propellers and the song of their engines. Each pilot hears the song of his own machine; he also hears the song of all, the song of the whole unit, the song of the Staffel.

Height: 1,500 metres. A red light suddenly flashes up in the bright afternoon sun. Nine pairs of eyes see it for an instant. Then it is gone.

Nine men know that the "hare" who is their protector has fired the red signal light as a warning to them.

Somewhere in the sky an enemy is lurking. Nine spell-bound,

fascinated pairs of eyes watch the hand of the leader pointing downwards. It points to north, east, south and west.

What is below them? What is above them?

Below them there is a huge, enormous, square, black something. A mass. It hovers almost motionless—a dark patch over the ground.

To left, to right, in front, behind—wherever they look, there are swarms of enemy scouts. No chaos, but a well-organised destiny. A destiny organised by men.

The black mass lying underneath the brown Fokkers is a closed, close-knit square of three hundred and twenty bombing machines, which have almost reached Bruges.

The mass lying above the Staffel is divided into many swarms. Enemy scouts are flying in every quarter of the heavens. There must be three hundred of them. All ready to dive.

The leader transmuted his thoughts into action while the nine pairs of eyes were still staring at him.

The nine men only saw his machine shoot downwards as straight as a plummet. Down at a fantastic speed, right into the midst of the black mass, into the enemy's square.

Nine men have no thoughts, for yesterday, today or tomorrow. Nine pilots push their sticks down and follow their chief.

The barrels of twice three hundred and twenty machine-guns are turned on to them from the cockpits of the enemy bombers.

Down go the nine at an incalculable speed, down into this hell.

Twice three hundred and twenty machine-guns are silent—petrified with amazement at this mad effort to scatter a formation of three hundred and twenty bombers.

A hellish din rises up from the ground beneath. Hundreds of anti-aircraft guns pour their screeching shrapnels into the air. A German Jagdstaffel—eleven green Fokkers—hastens to aid the death-scorning brown Fokkers.

Hundreds of anti-aircraft guns seem determined to prevent this help reaching them. They emit a fiery mass of iron into the air, but the helpers force a passage through this red-hot wall with uncanny immunity.

Three hundred and twenty bomber pilots have no idea what the thirty-five Germans charging into their midst intend to do. When they recover their wits, it is too late.

As if inspired by some supernatural power, fourteen blue naval Fokkers, ten brown and eleven green Fokkers have broken up a formation of three hundred and twenty opponents.

In the panic-like disorder which follows twice three hundred and twenty machine-guns can do nothing.

A furious battle commences. Three hundred enemy scouts are there to aid the bombing squadron in the fray.

Thirty-five against six hundred and twenty.

The fight is for Bruges. Tens of thousands of men wounded in the last offensive lie there, waiting for transport home.

Millions of cartridges, hundreds of thousands of shells and hand-grenades are stored in Bruges.

A civilian population of men, women and children lives in this town. But three hundred and twenty aeroplanes have come to drop their bombs on Bruges.

Thirty-five aeroplanes try with all their might, with all their will and with all their power to prevent them.

For them it is not a fight against six hundred and twenty enemy machines. It is a fight waged by the thirty-five for thousands of human lives which are the helpless prey of the deadly, devastating bombs.

Millions of flame-emitting shells, a howl and a roar—glides, dives, circles, turns and collisions—these constitute the fight in the air. A foretaste of the destruction of the world.

One flaming mass after another plunges headlong into the depths as burning wreckage. No one knows whether it is friend or foe. Each defending machine is engaged with forty, fifty, sixty opponents.

It all seems like the monstrous abortion of an erring humanity which has lost its God.

But the power which has been stored up is nigh to exhaustion. Fate has ordained that even the best-filled petrol tanks become empty at last.

After the fight has lasted for three-quarters of an hour the irony of Fate ordains imperiously that it shall end.

The survivors of the six hundred machines are emptied of their power. They are exhausted.

They have come to the end—to the end of today.

Three hundred and twenty bombing machines get rid of their loads of bombs so that they may reach their lines with the last remaining drops of their petrol. All these bombs miss their mark. They fall in the coppices and in the devastated woods, where they can do little damage to men or materials.

Bruges is saved.

The entry in the Jagdstaffel's book:

May 12th, 1918: air fight over Bruges.

Flying time and duration of the engagement: 45 minutes.

Destroyed: 21 bombing machines, 19 English and American scouting machines. 40 enemy aircraft landed in German territory.

Own casualties: 3 killed, 4 wounded.

CHAPTER XI

Lieutenant Olden was troubled. Not because the life of the Staffel had undergone any change in its regularity. Good Lord—that regularity!

Perhaps it was the real trouble. Up in the morning, front patrols, lunch, more front patrols while the others were overhauling their machines, concocting new plans and trying out ever more daring flights. Day followed day, days grew into months, months grew into years. Spring, summer, autumn and winter. Three and a half years.

Comrades fell; new men came, fitted themselves into their coterie, fought, died—there seemed no end to the invincible springs of life. There seemed no end to the invincible sea of death. New men came, with their souls already dominated by their uniforms; the men-machines guided the flying-machines. No new men came—only new names.

They came from a land that was hungry. They knew exactly what the front expected of them and did their duty to the best of their knowledge—but their nerves—those virile hardened nerves—rebelled. They rebelled against the deadly monotony of their work, which was so dangerous in a twofold sense. They meditated on the senselessness of their actions; they became fatalists; they grew apathetic to their own lot.

Perhaps the terrific odds of that battle over Bruges brought these vague feelings to a head. At all events they manifested themselves in a phenomenon which grew ever more frequent—"airweariness." Brains simply refused to function; they went on strike. Strantz was unable to fly; he forgot the simplest manipulations of the controls. The prince lay awake all night in bed; if he heard the slightest sound, he grasped his pistol and fired into the darkness, but the next morning he had no recollection of what he had done. Quarrels became the order of the day. Even the chief's black punishment book was impotent to put a check on the excessive drinking and smoking.

The last few days had brought air fights which could only be fought by men who possessed the strength of madness or had eliminated the last particle of nerve. Men from Europe, America, Asia, Africa and Australia were fighting for every foot's breadth of Europe. The brown Fokkers hurtled a bare ten metres above the tortured, trampled soil, across barbed-wire entanglements, over the heads of men who assailed one another with spades, knives and the butt-ends of rifles.

Hand grenades, flammerwerfers and machine-guns *ad infinitum*. And then the enemy's tanks—those dreaded spectral tanks from which bullets rebounded harmlessly as they reeled forward, ever forward, over the bodies of men, over barbed-wire entanglements, through shell-holes, through standing water and then over the bodies of men again. And then the gas! The poison!

Ten, fifteen, twenty metres overhead flew the scouts, with full petrol tanks and ammunition belts. Their wings whistled as they raged along the lines of the trenches, where almost every bullet fired into the thick masses of infantrymen awaiting the signal to attack found a billet. What cover was there for them? What use were even their concreted dugouts? All the soldiers of the trenches were possessed of the impotent fury of the man who was defenceless against the foeman of the air.

American and English scouts dive down on to the brown Fokkers at twenty, thirty, forty metres. Words fail to depict the courage, the despair, the hatred. There is nothing human in the screams of the men. Their brains are dazed with the din of bursting shells.

The war has become a competition between the designers' offices. It is a certainty that every new type of aircraft put into action today will be over-trumped next week; never have the technical powers of the inventors been so keyed up as in these three and a half years. The means of protection adopted by the armies on the ground cannot stay this pace; the men become ever more defenceless, and the greater the weakening of their morale, the greater must be the effort to combat it.

Dulce et decorum est pro patria mori.

Lieutenant Olden is troubled. His pilots, yes, his pilots must be freed from this incubus. His comradeship with them would be incomplete if he let matters rest as they were.

But—have not he and all the men of his unit the best of lives compared with their comrades in the trenches? Every man in it has a bed, water to wash himself and his food and drink. And the men in the trenches?

Has the chief really any right to be troubled?

An American bombing squadron.

CHAPTER XII

It was obvious that Kussin and Hamann had to tell the others about the Café Leonidas. It was equally obvious that they said nothing about their failure to conquer the ladies there.

Once again the days of rest drew near. The prospect of spending thirty-six hours in this paradise quelled all the quarrels. The chief breathed freely again and praised the resourcefulness of the fattest and the youngest members of his Staffel.

They all wanted to visit the Café Leonidas. The Staffel did everything in common, and there was no jealousy. Comrades in the air, and comrades on the ground!

Over breakfast Olden counted up the amounts amassed by the black punishment book during the last month. The total sum was a pleasant one, because, as usual, it was to furnish the basis of the excursion's expenses.

The prince had struck up a good friendship with the cook, and whenever there was chocolate pudding, he told so many stories before the meal that they all lost their appetites; then he ate all of his favourite dish alone and with the greatest relish. It cannot be denied that it cost him twenty-five marks, for offences such as smacking the lips and speaking with the mouth full had their fixed penalties.

"More than three hundred marks—that's a huge lot!" Steffen

threw a glance across his shoulder in the chief's direction.

"If our parents only knew!"

"Yes, if they only knew how their darlings were getting on!"

There was a perceptible quaver in Rom's voice, for Steffen's jest had become bitter earnest to him.

"Oh, come, come!" said Mierdl propitiatingly, "perhaps some nice little girl will give you a new mascot!"

"Mascots are always old," Kussin instructed him.

"You, there, who's the chap who wouldn't fly for a couple of days because his silk nightcap had disappeared? And who's the chap who now puts his trust in the protective efforts of the new nightcap which your good kind Johann Georg brought along from Ghent?" The prince's eye-glass gleamed as he mocked. "Man alive, you wouldn't be flying today if it wasn't for that!"

General laughter. Kussin went pale with anger. "And you with your bit of glass! How many dozen victories has it brought you? It's only a bit of window-glass!"

"Well, what about it?" the prince shouted back at him. "I find it quite all right. I can see you better through my window-pane."

"If you're going to spend the whole thirty-six hours shouting at each other, I'm off!" The chief stood in the doorway as he spoke. He was just back from the men's canteen, for he always wanted them to have their fun, too, when he and his pilots went away to amuse themselves. It is often more difficult to receive than to give, as the chief knew well enough, and some people can be very sensitive. But today there was a very good reason, for his clerk Lehmann beamed as he told him of the birth of his fifth offspring. So all the men could have their beer today, because two hundred and sixty marks would see the pilots through, and he could allow the men forty marks from the education fund as well, and another ten from his own purse. He hoped all the good wishes expressed on the beer-stained field-postcards consigned to Munich would form a good omen for the future life of the new little Lehmann!

Chief Olden—the father of Jagdstaffel 356!

The Café Leonidas overtopped all expectations. The prince was full of charm and all-conquering amiability; he quite forgot his eyeglass and his blasé tone. Olden bought ten new pairs of socks, Rom some gloriously scented soap, Hamann a new patent leather belt, Mierdl some new music and Strantz some old Burgundy.

The red coconut matting was stormed and proclaimed German territory. Rom sang the Lorelei in a melodious bass, and Kussin wept bitter tears to it.

Later on they all danced, and the orchestra played the Wedding March conscientiously. The red velvet curtain lost all its terrors; the proprietor and the waiters beamed.

The chief also beamed. He did not dance; he sat quietly in his corner because his *Pour le Mérite* forbade him to join the mirthful noisy throng—the gossip of the base is so swift and merciless in its effects. He smoked and drank and went far towards forgetting his troubles.

Later on in the evening came Madame Jeanette, as the waiters called her. She was the mysterious, proud, icy-cold beauty of whom Hamann and Kussin had related such wonderful tales. But there was really nothing wonderful or mysterious about Madame Jeanette, although the tale of her and Lieutenant Olden cannot be told here. That was the only secret he kept from his comrades. It is a secret belonging to that indescribably beautiful world of two persons which is always silently present, even in the midst of war's alarms. That is the secret and wonderful tale of Madame Jeanette and Lieutenant Olden.

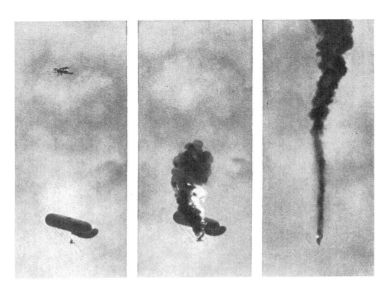

Above: A SUCCESSFUL ATTACK ON A BALLOON
Below: A GERMAN BALLOON

Chapter XIII

The peace of night is over the front. Signal rockets gleam afar, rise up to heaven and fall in sparkling drops on the broad dark landscape. Here and there a searchlight flashes out; there is a dull rumble of the heavy guns at Verdun.

Baumann cannot sleep. The chief is not back yet. If anyone goes off alone on a front flight and does not land again within seventy-five minutes, the whole Staffel goes to look for him and a telephone message goes through to the front line to make enquiries. When he has been absent for an hour and a half, a cross is put against his name—dead or missing!

The chief took off last night, with the intention of paying a visit to the neighbouring Staffel, but he ought to have been back long ago. Yes, long ago! But really nothing could have happened to him on the way to the neighbouring Staffel. Engine trouble is out of the question, because he, Baumann, is the most reliable of all mechanics. He knows that as surely as he knows his own name. Olden must have been detained for some reason and spent the night with the green Fokkers. Baumann has been waiting six hours for him. How many periods of ninety minutes does that make?

He is sitting with the paymaster, who has just returned from leave, and retailing him the events of the last fortnight. "Not so long ago an American bomber came across when it was as dark as it is now, and you should have seen the lads take off! Mother of God, they were all in their nightshirts! Lieutenant Hans and his green Fokkers were up after that big pantechnicon too, likewise in their nightshirts!" Baumann choked with laughter. "And my chief and Hans forced the Yanks down on to our aerodrome after they had left their visiting cards on the tool-sheds!"

"God in Heaven," sighed the paymaster, "that'll mean a pretty bill for repairs!"

"I daresay," replied Baumann, "so you'd better get hold of a bit of money! But the American crew was shunted off—they all had a booze first—and then we kept their undamaged machine here. It carries five men—well, what follows?"

The paymaster shook a perplexed head.

"Why, man alive, Hans said just before he took off: 'Now you can all fly to Brussels in it and see your girls'!"

The paymaster laughed and yawned. "I say, it's getting light again, and the chief isn't back yet!"

The silence that fell on the two men became uncanny. Every word they spoke seemed to resound through the room.

So they went out to the aerodrome, which was still wet with the morning dew. Baumann searched the horizon with his glasses. Day came quickly. The shy voices of the birds grew louder; a lorry column rumbled heavily along the road.

One pilot after another arrived shiveringly; only the chief was missing. They all stood looking westwards.

"There—be quiet—can't you hear anything?" They bent their heads to listen. "That's the chief!" They heard the hum of a propeller grow clearer.

"That's him! But what's up? Why's he going down behind the wood?"

"Car!" roared Baumann. "Ambulance car!"

"He's climbing again! Since when do you land downwind?"

Baumann left the excited pilots standing there. He jumped on the ambulance car and directed it towards the machine that was taxiing slowly onward.

They found Olden huddled in his seat, with his face distorted by pain. "Herr Lieutenant," shouted Baumann, "what's up?"

"Shot through the heel—Sopwith——" he muttered, and his head fell on to the instrument board.

The pilots hastened to the scene, seated in cars or clinging to the running-boards. They jumped down. The chief was wounded—the chief! Not even behind the front was anyone safe from those Sopwiths!

But Baumann already had a foot on the machine's step; he kicked at the bracing wires until he found a foothold. Then he undid the safety belt carefully and lifted the now unconscious pilot out. "Chief, chief, where did you get it? In the heel? Holy Mary and Joseph help me! Oh, the swine! Our chief!" He gave vent to uncontrollable lamentation.

No mother could have tended her son more lovingly than the giant Baumann cared for the small, fragile Olden. Heedless of the pilots, he laid him on the stretcher himself; in the ambulance he dictated the speed to the driver, whom he threatened with a mighty thrashing if he shook the chief up too much on the rough road. The car containing the horrified pilots followed close behind.

When they reached the hospital, Baumann took the chief in his arms and carried him up the steps, past all the orderlies and nurses.

"Tell the doctor to come at once," he ordered.

Without further ado he carried the unconscious man into the operating theatre. There he remained standing in the doorway, deaf to all the requests and persuasions of the doctors who wanted him to go. He watched their preparations with a suspicious eye, and refused admission to the pilots who had bounded up the stairs with mighty leaps and now stood panting behind him. His eyes followed mistrustfully every movement of the nurses who cut Olden's boots and breeches off and of the staff-surgeon, who continually washed and dried his hands.

The anaesthetic mask descended upon Olden's face.

"Hell! Get out now, or you're for the cells!" The doctor lost patience. Never before had he had the experience of being told by a hairy-faced Bavarian how he was to handle a wounded man.

But Baumann had the last word. His face was red and his fists were clenched when the hospital orderlies pushed him out, but they heard his voice through the closed doors.

"This I'll tell you, doctor," he roared, "if the chief pegs out, you're going to peg out too!"

CHAPTER XIV

Theory and practice: The first American bombing squadrons which came to Europe preferred to fly in a square formation. Not until some time later did they adopt the V formation which had become almost a tradition at the front.

Theory and practice: The pilots knew their sectors as well as they knew themselves. It is true that their maps were re-marked daily and identification marks were displayed for their benefit in the front-line trenches, but they knew the lines, the quagmires and the shell-holes. They knew their areas by day or night. Who wants to study a map when engaged in an air fight!

All the newly-arrived Americans received general staff maps marked up to date. The time came for them to make their first flights. They received much good advice and many warnings. They had all learnt to fly and shoot well; they were young and ambitious.

Nine Americans take off. They become involved in a fight over the lines. They acquit themselves well, but the course of the fray carries them far away beyond the positions of which they know only too little.

They have sustained no losses. When the Germans have disengaged, they close up in a model "swarming duck" formation and fly back across the lines, hardly worried at all by a few Archie clouds. Far and wide there is no enemy aircraft in sight.

Nine raw American pilots see beneath them an aerodrome equipped with landing-mark and wind sock. They go down. Not a soul in sight. They land upwind in the regulation manner. All nine of them.

A brief burst of machine-gun fire suddenly whistles over their heads and buries itself in the sand. As if conjured out of the soil, German Landsturmers bear down upon the bewildered Americans. More and more Germans make their appearance. The greater their numbers, the greater is the bewilderment of the Americans.

An English-speaking officer explains the tragi-comic situation to them. In their ignorance of the district the Americans have lost their way. They have landed on an emergency landing-ground close behind the German lines, under the assumption that it was one of their own.

They were almost weeping with rage at the thought of having to surrender without a fight. They were in despair as they stood beside their trim machines, but they could do nothing except count the number of hits on them.

A telephone message went through to the pilots of the brown Fokkers, who arrived in their cars and invited the American comrades to pass the time with them until the intelligence officer arrived.

The nine American machines were a sensation for the Staffel. They were built of first-class materials; they glittered with nickel and brass; their clocks had luminous hands; everything about them was new and practical and the best peace-time work. The same applied to their uniforms; they wore thick, heavy leather overcoats and wonderful boots—all made regardless of expense.

Nineteen young men experienced a few jolly hours together. The Americans sang their war-songs, and the Germans sang theirs. They sang and drank the whole night through, and in the morning the brown Fokkers took off to wreak more death and destruction.

If those nineteen lads—all about the same age—had not worn different uniforms and spoken different languages, there would have been practically no difference between them. Yet anyone who scanned them closely would have noted more vivacity and less strain on the American faces. The War which they had travelled thousands of miles to take part in had not lasted a week for them. Perhaps an ironical Fate had saved them from the experiences which had robbed their German hosts of their youth long ago.

Chapter XV

For the space of five weeks pilots and mechanics visited their chief. A waiting list was drawn up, so that everyone should have his turn. They brought the finest and dearest grapes that could be found in Brussels, they gathered books and borrowed gramophone records for the old wheezy hospital instrument. Baumann tramped for hours in his efforts to discover half a litre of real Bavarian beer, while the cook roasted a young chicken every now and then and wrapped it up carefully. He also sealed the wrappings lest the carrier should experience any too great desire to have a taste of it.

They related to him every fight and even the smallest incidents.

Rom took his place to the best of his ability, but what was Jagdstaffel 356 without its Lieutenant Olden? Merely a wreck!

And then, one day, the chief was back again. He hobbled along on a crutch, with his wounded foot encased in a slipper. The Red Cross sister who accompanied him laid repeated stress on the fact that this was only a short visit which the staff-surgeon had granted most exceptionally to satisfy the constant pleadings of the patient, who was due to spend another fortnight in hospital.

Flowers made a sudden appearance on the mess table. Hamann shouted for champagne. The cook entered with the chief's favourite

86

dish—omelette and cranberries. Where he managed to get the cranberries was an unsolved problem to all of them.

The works foreman mustered the mechanics on the aerodrome. The news of the chief's arrival spread itself with the speed of the wind.

Then at last the chief stood before them, looking somewhat smaller and more fragile than usual; he stood there with his crutch and slipper and was most embarrassed when he made a brief speech. Afterwards he went with them to the canteen, where there was a wonderful opportunity for free beer; the chief had to clink glasses with every man of them. The works foreman called for three cheers for the chief, after which Rom and the prince made a saddle of their hands and carried him to the tarmac. The Red Cross sister followed like a shadow.

The streamers of leadership were already swaying on the chief's Fokker. Baumann lifted him into his seat. The Red Cross sister fluttered like a hen alarmed for her chicks.

"I protest, Herr Lieutenant! The Herr Staff-Surgeon will have a fit. There are bound to be complications!"

"I only want to open up the engine," said Olden ingratiatingly.

"I protest!" repeated the unhappy girl.

"Carry on with your protests, Fraulein!" shouted the prince above the roar of the engine. "We all believe we may assume you to be a Protestant." The mighty roar of laughter mingled with the whirr of the revolving propeller. The chief found no difficulty in making an elegant take-off with one foot in a boot and the other in a slipper over the bandages.

First one brown Fokker took off and then another, until at last all the comrades were in the air, with the chief heading the formation, as was fitting.

They flew to Ypres and counted the Archie cloudlets there, but soon turned back. When they were about to land they saw Sister

Anna with the crutch and a brandy flask, standing on the aerodrome beside Baumann who carried his field-glasses as usual. Baumann had made several attempts to combat Sister Anna's fainting fits with the brandy, but all in vain.

CHAPTER XVI

The staff-surgeon stirred his coffee cup thoughtfully. How was he to make it clear to this thick-skulled Bavarian that he would perhaps do his Staffel more harm than good by remaining at the front during his convalescence? How could he possibly establish a special department of his hospital for him, especially when he was so short-handed? A mad world! There were plenty of men who did not want to leave the hospital, but here was one who simply would not stay in it!

"My dear fellow," he said, staring at Olden with his shortsighted, inflamed eyes, "you are wasting my time in a positively shameless way! If all my patients gave me so much trouble, I'd have been dead long ago. Well, to cut it short, I'll make you a proposal. Get yourself transferred to Farmars for a few weeks and drill the future scout-fliers there. Quite a nice amusing job for you, but you've got to relax a bit and clear out of this mess at the front for a while!"

"Now listen, doctor! Are you really so innocent, or are you just putting it on? Have you ever trotted over from Valenciennes to Farmars to see what goes on there? No, you haven't, or you wouldn't give me such advice!"

The doctor was about to lose his temper. He tried to think of the right swear words to use.

"I'll tell you a tale from my experiences as an airman. You can guess for yourself how many pounds of weight our good friend Höhne lost on that occasion." Olden saw the doctor glance at his watch and laughed. "Got enough coffee in your cup? Good!

"Well, you know Lieutenant Höhne; he's the last survivor of the original Boelcke Staffel. He's the boss of the Jagdstaffel school at Farmars, where he thus places his great experience at the service of the young pilots who have to be trained. Once there were ten of us pupils there, and we thought we were mighty fine pilots. Well, in the early hours of our first morning there Höhne initiated us into the secrets of the huntsmen of the air. Each of us had to climb into the one-seater Pfalz; Höhne buckled him into his belt himself and showed him how to unbuckle it with one movement, how to put the fore and middle fingers correctly on the trigger-buttons of the machine-guns, how to handle the controls in a vertically banked turn when the machine goes over on to one wing-tip at an angle of ninety degrees, how the functions of rudder and elevator interchange in such cases, etc. Then we had to fly a trial round of the aerodrome. As soon as Höhne fired off a signal light, the pupil had to pull his machine round in a vertically banked turn without losing height."

"I don't see why that should be such an exciting business for the instructor," the doctor interjected.

"Just you wait!" The chief smiled. "Höhne was very sorry for himself, because the business is by no means so simple as it looks. 'More snap into it, gentlemen, more snap!' he was always saying. And then there were landings when the machine stood on her nose, and crumpled undercarriages, and broken props. and broken bones as well. But the sharpshooting was a really nasty business. They put up a target in the middle of the aerodrome—three metres high by two wide—and behind it in a shelter there are several mechanics to mark your hits.

"There's a Pfalz waiting for you, with thirty rounds in its two guns. You're told to climb to 1,000 metres, go into a turn, shoot off a green signal light and then, as soon as you see a white one fired from the ground, put your machine into a nose-dive, no matter what position it happens to be in at the moment, and go down on the target. Then you put the Pfalz into the line of fire, score 27 hits on the target at 30 metres' distance, pull your machine up again and land. You can't be certain of hitting anything farther off than 30 metres, you know.

"Well, you try diving down 970 metres and then putting 27 shots on to a target with a diameter of two metres. As a matter of fact, all the bullets went spurting on the sand, because none of us got any nearer to the target than 100 metres. 'Get down to it,' shouted Höhne, 'get right down to it, you wash-outs!' I tried it three or four times, and then I lost my Bavarian temper. The armoury master gave my guns another thirty rounds apiece, and I took off. Climb to 1,000. Green signal light. White one flashes up from the ground. I put the machine on to her nose; my wings shudder, the bracing wires whistle, the ground jumps up towards me, the target swells up from a tiny point to a big patch, so that I can see the black rings on it. I get nearer to it, put in my thirty rounds, pull the stick hard, open up my engine—and then I hear an almighty crack, like a house tumbling to pieces. My Pfalz is thrown up into the air and I get a hell of a shaking, so that I think I'll be dead the next minute. I just have enough strength to fly a couple of circles, and look overboard. But where's the bally target? There was a big white target there just now, but it's gone—it's been blown to bits! I fly up to the landing-mark, and there stands Höhne, white as a sheet and waving both his arms about. A mechanic keeps on shooting off red danger signals, and one of my messmates is holding up a wheel. That wheel was all that remained of my undercarriage, and can you tell me, dear doctor, how one lands without an undercarriage?"

The doctor muttered something unintelligible.

"Cold shivers went down my back as I realised what had happened. I'd rammed that target and bashed both it and my undercarriage to smithereens. Oh, I was in a hell of a funk as I waited for the moment when my machine was going to break up!

"I flew round the aerodrome. I saw an ambulance. That was for me. But I'd got to land somehow first! I wondered what they'd say in my obituary notice; 'accidentally killed in a practice flight,' I supposed. But I realised it was no good thinking about such things and so went down to land.

"Höhne was standing up in his car, watching my heroic efforts. I dropped down a bit and could see his body go limp. The ambulance buzzed off to the spot where it thought I was going to land, but when I saw the red cross on it, no, I couldn't do it. I pulled my stick up again and started flying round the aerodrome again. I can't tell you how many times I went round—ten at least, probably something nearer twenty. Again and again I tried to land, but each time I funked it. I could imagine what would happen when I landed, and it was ghastly. I should have been flying round that aerodrome still; I didn't want to come down at all, but I ran out of petrol. The engine stopped, sputtered a couple of times, and the prop went slower and slower. So I pushed my stick down and went into a steep turn to keep the way on the machine, but she side-slipped! I had just enough presence of mind at the last moment to unbuckle my safety belt; I pulled my knees up instinctively and put my hands up to protect my face. Then there was a cracking and a splintering, and my head began to hum. An invisible hand chucked me up into the air; I shot off in a long parabola and landed in the sand. I jerked myself up with the last remnants of my ebbing strength and started running for all I was worth. I heard a bang behind me, and there was the Pfalz blazing away.

"Höhne didn't know whether to laugh or cry. He wanted to laugh because I was more or less safe and sound, and he was pretty well in tears at seeing his lovely Pfalz go the way of all flesh. But I was excused all further target practice, and Höhne swore the business had turned his hair grey. Dear Dr. Schneider, you're not going to ask me to apply for that sort of job, are you?"

"No, Olden, you're right there! So you'd better stay on here, and we'll manage your treatment somehow."

An orderly announced the arrival of the staff-surgeon's car.

"Well, *au revoir*, my dear Olden. My enforced visit to you and the tale you told me have lost me so much time that there's going to be no sleep for me tonight. There are three hundred and forty-seven patients and twenty-eight overworked nurses waiting for me. Do you know what that means, to look after three hundred and forty-seven badly wounded men who can't be sent back—and what sort of wounds, too? No, you simply haven't an idea of that, and your flying is child's play to my job!" He paused at the door and turned back. "Has it ever occurred to you what a mad time we're living in? Mad isn't the word for it; we have to invent another one."

FOKKER DVII. *Photo courtesy of Norman Franks*

Chapter XVII

The distant Flanders sky was slightly overcast. Rom and the chief flew along the enemy's lines at a comparatively low height. They could easily distinguish the front line with its breastworks and barbed-wire entanglements and the narrow, winding communication trenches leading up to it.

"How primitive mankind has grown again!" thought Rom. "They are turning into cavemen, like they were hundreds of thousands of years ago, but in those days man fought man hand to hand, and now we do it all from a distance. Progress or retrogression? Well, our comrades down there haven't any time to worry about such things! How well my engine is working today! Glorious to be in the air! Alone! Such a big, wide world! And I'm floating about between heaven and earth! Where are their boundaries?" A gust shook the machine. "What silly ideas you get! You've got to look out, my lad! There's madness waiting for you down below there! And what's up above me? Perhaps the enemy is waiting for me high above the clouds, and higher up still there's God waiting for us! Is He waiting for us? Well, I'm off on leave tomorrow!" That was the last link in Rom's chain of thoughts.

They flew down towards Kemmel. A French balloon rose a

couple of hundred metres above the ground, from which altitude it directed the heavy artillery on to the landscape which had already been so devastated by the drum fire.

Drum fire! Mountains that belch flame for days and nights on end, glowing masses of iron, volcanoes of horror, hells of dread. And yet the men on both sides, friend and foe, can stand it. Today, they think, will be the end, but tomorrow the end becomes a new beginning.

Rom sees the chief's Fokker close before him. A hole in the clouds reveals a patch of blue sky. They are high enough to be out of Archie's range.

The chief turns round and points to the right with his hand. Rom searches the horizon. Nothing to be seen—and yet—now—three Sopwiths. Their rotary engines look like huge fish-mouths, while the wings resemble thin silver threads.

The two Germans change their course. Rom grasps the pull-rings of his machine-guns more firmly.

They charge ahead.

Two English machines make off when the Fokkers approach. Out of petrol, probably.

Rom climbs a hundred metres.

The remaining Sopwith hurtles towards them. The streamers of leadership flutter from its wings. A squadron commander!

Rom bends over to look at the chief. Two leaders fighting one another. He circles round to wait and watch.

The Sopwith and the Fokker charge one another like fighting-cocks. Olden opens his throttle. Now he is in the line of fire. The fish-mouth comes into his sights.

The German—at twenty metres' distance—fires in sharp short bursts.

The Englishman—at twenty metres' distance—fires in sharp short bursts.

"Damn!" thinks Olden, "missed him!" He pulls his machine round to the right in a steep turn—*huiiiii!* sing the bracing wires. "I've still four hundred shots left, and the English machine's got to know that today!" A duel between two leaders!

The chief fires—but—he can hear nothing—only the whirr of the propeller.

English bullets howl as they pierce the wings.

Olden's face is distorted—a gun jam! His two machine-guns have jammed. He clenches his teeth, his eyes are bloodshot.

The English streamers!

He goes into a turn; he tries again. But the jam is still there.

The Sopwith follows him, but its guns are silent. The English pilot bends overboard and waves to the German. He knows the bad luck of jammed guns only too well. He puts his hand to his helmet in greeting—a true scout will fight no defenceless pilots. He goes into a turn and makes for the English lines.

To Rom his turn is a signal to attack. He charges after the Sopwith with an open throttle. If the chief can't do it, he will!

Olden pursues like a storm wind. His machine must give him the utmost today. The maximum revolutions—for Rom will catch up the Englishman in a few moments.

Olden pulls his stick up; the leap takes him over his comrade's head. A left turn brings him into Rom's line of flight. He waves and roars: "Don't shoot, don't attack—gun jammed!"

Rom waves back. He has understood.

The two brown Fokkers turn homeward.

Olden's pent-up rage was discharged on the armoury master and mechanics. They hardly knew their chief, who was always so quiet.

"I'm off on leave tomorrow!" thinks Rom.

The following morning an English machine flies over the German aerodrome at a great height and goes down in corkscrew turns. The Archies raise their long barrels. The enemy dives down to within two hundred metres, catches his machine, fires a signal light and drops a message. There is a note in the bag to which the long red, white and blue streamers are attached. "It means you or me by our next meeting. Strats, Captain"

Rom went off. The prince took over his solitary patrols. But Olden could think of nothing but Captain Strats. You or me. One of us two. The fish-mouth or the brown Fokker.

Olden and the prince take off for Kemmel. Hand-to-hand encounters are raging below them. They want to bring that balloon down; they must have it. They keep their eyes fixed on the horizon, for somewhere there can and will be a foeman lurking for them. What goes on five hundred metres below them must be no concern of theirs now.

To northward there lies a German naval squadron flying in close formation, to east of them there are English contact patrols, while over yonder there appear to be English scouts.

Olden is far away to southward, heading for the balloon. And now the naval Fokkers turn off eastward. The contact patrol machines are deep in their own hinterland, where they slowly vanish from view.

The prince listens to the monotonous song of his engine. It occurs to him that there must be thirteen German machines in the air now. Thirteen! No—no good being superstitious! Thirteen! Silly!

Where is the chief? Still round Kemmel way? They seem to have hauled that balloon down! In broad daylight, too?

A short sharp burst of machine-gun fire makes him jerk his head up. A Sopwith has dived down on him suddenly; its pilot shoots, goes into a narrow turn and shoots again.

The prince goes into a turn with his engine full on—aims—shoots—hits! Fokker and Sopwith hurtle past one another. The Sopwith carries a leader's streamers—Strats! Captain Strats! Thirteen! Thirteen! Thirteen!

The chief charges up. The prince can recognise the set look on his face. Then he climbs.

The fire from the English machine-guns flashes up after him. The blue phosphorus hisses. The prince hears the thud of the hits in his Fokker.

Olden dives down on to his opponent, fires—misses. The bullets whistle. Olden goes into a turn and attacks again.

"Where did the fellow hit me?" The prince becomes aware of an intense heat. There is something wrong. His engine is working, but—thirteen—thirteen—thirteen!

And now—Strats is going to ram him—without a second's pause the prince pulls his stick up. The machine wobbles and threatens to stall.

It is damnably hot!

He looks overboard. Far away down below Strats is tearing away, with Olden at his heels. The prince goes into a turn—and in the turn a jet of flame shoots out from the engine and flashes close past his head. Another flame licks the side of his cockpit and hisses along to the steering surfaces. The Fokker is on fire!

"My Fokker is on fire!" The prince roars and screams. "I must get out, must get out!"

He glances at his altimeter, but it is shot to pieces.

Then, while his right hand loosens his safety belt, his left gropes to his seat, for the cord of his parachute is fastened to a hook on the steel tubing which forms a rest for his back. He presses his knees against the stick.

All this is a matter of seconds. He stands up on his seat, with his parachute pack pushing against the hollows of his knees. Then the wind stream set up by the increasing pace of the machine's fall pulls him along the fuselage.

The prince is falling. Head foremost. He has only one thought: will the parachute open? He counts—twenty-one, twenty-two—can seconds really be so long? Twenty-three, twenty-four—his nerves are in shreds! Down he goes head foremost. The parachute must open—it was tested before he took off—twenty-five, twenty-six—it is his only hope of safety! Thirteen—thirteen—thirteen!

A sharp jolt pulls him round; his head is jerked up; the blood rushes to his ears. A loud report—and then he seems to be standing still in the air. The prince sways slowly earthward.

Below him he sees his machine, a fiery red mass, with a long black trail of smoke behind him. He dare not think of his end if he had remained in that glowing, seething mass! But Olden still hurtles after the Sopwith. The strong west wind has driven the combatants far into German territory.

The prince glides down slowly and safely.

Now Strats goes into a turn with a dead propeller. The chief is close above him and continues to force him down.

The prince can feel his heart beating. He still feels the after-effects of those last minutes. It was touch and go for him. He dare not make the slightest movement for fear he should slip out of his parachute-belt.

A German Fokker appears on the horizon.

Strats has flattened out to land; Olden is close behind him. Then —the Sopwith overturns. Will it bury the captain beneath its wreckage? Thank Heaven, the chief has done the job!

The Fokker is quite close; it is a brown one. Kussin—good old Kussin! He waves. Never in his life has the prince felt so grateful to anyone as when he sees Kussin circling round and protecting him.

The parachute drifts towards the solitary, lonely wall of a house which has been destroyed by shell-fire. Kussin calls and waves, but the prince cannot understand him, for he is exhausted. He only sees the ruin looming up towards him—growing into something enormous—he feels the impact as he meets it—and then nothing more.

Kussin fires a red signal light, but some sappers who have noticed the parachute's descent hasten on the scene and release the pilot.

A slight concussion, some slight burns and some skin scraped off are the visible signs of the prince's last quarter of an hour.

Kussin speeds to the aerodrome, where he warns the others and chases up some cars. Several of them go off to fetch the chief and Strats, while others seek the hero of the parachute descent.

"Have you brought me an eye-glass?" were the first words the prince spoke when he recovered consciousness.

"Weeds never die," said Hamann drily. "Here you are!"

The prince placed it to his eye; a laugh spread over his grimed, smoke-blackened face. He looked at his friends. "Boys, you don't know how jolly it is to be alive," he said.

They all arrived back about the same time. Strats congratulated the prince, whose single burst had been his Sopwith's undoing.

The prince in turn congratulated Strats for having shot him down. Both congratulated the chief, whose obstinate pursuit had compelled Strats to land. They were all chivalrous opponents!

Strats, who was a tall, blond Canadian, spoke German fluently, having studied at Bonn before the War. The Staffel kept this mighty foeman as its guest for forty-eight hours. He was a splendid comrade—very proud of his nation and unsurpassed in the telling of airmen's tales. He paid Jagdstaffel 356 a tribute of unstinted admiration, but he and his new-found German friends tactfully avoided any topic which might assail the honour of their respective countries, and not a single word was spoken about the strategic situation. The mutual respect of airmen was something above the conflict of nations.

When Strats departed, he presented his mascot to the prince. It was a golliwog with a silk ribbon round its neck, and had been salved from his machine. The ribbon was a gift from a lady of Paris.

FOKKER DVII (POSTWAR). *Photo courtesy of Norman Franks*

Chapter XVIII

Rom came back from his leave. He was tired, worn out and full of presentiments of death.

The chief took him to task.

"Rom, what's happened to you at home? Look here, old boy, we've been so long together in Flanders—tell me what's up?"

"I often went over to Schleissheim and had a look at the flying school. I couldn't be all that time without a machine!"

"Yes. Well?"

"That tall navy chap is an instructor there," Rom told him. "He thought I ought to put in for a transfer to home service. I've come through three and a half years of it here safely, he said, but one day there's an end of your luck. He's right!"

"Rom, you're air-tired; that's all. Do you remember the time when I couldn't fly for five days and funked my landings? Yes, you may laugh! I got over it all right. We've all had that sort of trouble!"

"I know my number's up soon, chief!"

He uttered these words so quietly and with such conviction that Older stared at him in amazement. "Rom, dear old Rom, you've hundreds of front patrols behind you, and you've always come back safe."

"Yes, that's it! You can do a hundred, and then the hundred first finishes you. I know it, Olden; I'm sure."

The chief stared out of the window. He could think of no reply. How could anyone of them know whether he would be alive tomorrow?

Rom stood motionless behind him. "I must talk him out of this," thought the chief, "or he'll infect me with his presentiments. But it's all nonsense! Unstrung nerves! Result of going on leave! Old women's gabble!" He turned round quickly.

There was an obstinate, veiled look on his comrade's face. For a long time the chief's eyes strove to read the riddle of that face.

"He won't listen to me," thought the chief sadly. "He won't listen to any of his friends!" And then aloud: "You'd better go now! Knock off flying for a couple of days. Have a good rest and get all the sleep you can!"

Rom left the room without a word.

"And suppose he's right? But what can I do?" Olden buried his head in his hands. What if Rom was right? But who can tell such things? Who indeed?

Rom did not fly for four days. He listened to the chaffing of the others with a friendly smile.

On the fifth day they were all going to Ypres. Suddenly Rom appeared on the aerodrome, carrying his helmet and glasses. "I'm coming along," he called out.

"We'll take you in the middle of the formation," said Olden, with a nod. "You see, you'll have got over your trouble in half an hour's time."

They took off. Rom's Fokker followed them in its usual place.

They flew to Ypres. Shrapnels shot up to them—but Rom's machine flew quietly onward. There was no sign of enemy aircraft; after half an hour's flight the chief turned homeward. They all looked at Rom, rejoicing at the thought that he was now his old self again, and all was well.

The chief flattened out to land first. Rom followed him. He

had taken off hundreds of times from that aerodrome; hundreds of times he had landed on it. Each time he had to fly over the embankment, two metres high, which surrounded it.

Slowly Rom's Fokker flattens out. He waves to his waiting mechanics, but miscalculates the height. His undercarriage charges into the embankment; he opens his throttle and tries to pull his machine up. But he is too low. His propeller touches the ground; the machine tips over, and his snapped propeller blades bore their way into the sand.

Rom is hurled out and remains lying on the ground, with a gaping rent in his skull. Splashes of his brains are left clinging to the machine.

CHAPTER XIX

They all kept step. There were eight pilots, headed by the Staffel-leader and the divisional chaplain, and then the long ranks of mechanics. They marched in a slow, measured time, which was dictated to them by the band playing the solemn, long-drawn strains of Chopin's Funeral March.

Many new wooden crosses were added to the numerous crosses of the cemetery.

Once again they stood by an open grave; once again the chaplain addressed them. They did not follow his words too closely. They were all thoroughly hardened, but today all their faces were white.

Rom! How old was he? Nineteen and a half years! He had taken part in hundreds of hard fights; each time he proudly counted the bullet holes in the wings of his brown Fokker. Once there were a hundred and thirty-two. One hundred and thirty-two steel-cased bullets hit his machine, but none of them touched him!

They did not follow the chaplain's words too closely, but never perhaps since their childhood's days were their feelings so devout as at the moment when the Paternoster resounded in the cemetery.

The chief threw three handfuls of earth in the grave; the band struck up "I had a comrade once . . ." All Rom's comrades—pilots and mechanics alike—threw three handfuls of earth into the grave, muttering a few kindly words.

Suddenly a German anti-aircraft battery in the neighbourhood began to thunder. Shrapnels hissed up to the sky incessantly.

A Sopwith appeared in the midst of the white cloudlets and went down on to the grave in a vertical dive. The anti-aircraft battery fired ever more furiously. Then the English pilot shot a red signal light, put his machine down as low as he could and dropped something.

It was a wreath of beech leaves, with long red, white and blue streamers. On one of them was written: "To the brave enemy the last regards."

The Sopwith circled round the grave several times at a low height and then turned off westwards. The chief raised his hand in salute; all the comrades followed his example. They did not lower their hands until the Englishman had disappeared on the horizon.

Then the chief dropped the wreath into Rom's grave.

Later on, statements made by prisoners informed them that the English had heard of Rom's death when they listened in to German telephone messages. The pilots of each sector—friend and foe— all knew one another from many fights in the air.

ALBATROS SCOUT LANDING. *Photo courtesy of Norman Franks*

Chapter XX

The chief stood on the aerodrome, with a couple of mechanics. It was reported to him that too little petrol had been delivered, and he wanted to look into the matter.

A troop of infantry passed by on the road. They came from the front-line trenches and were on their way to rest billets. They were dirty; their eyes were bleary.

They had a few lightly wounded men with them. The white of their emergency dressings formed a vivid contrast to their shabby uniforms.

Slowly and heavily this little group of humanity passed on its way.

The mechanics paused from their work. They were all elderly men, Landsturmers, whose ages were double those of their pilots. They knew the difference between an aerodrome and a front-line trench sufficiently well; at times they suffered from attacks by enemy bombing squadrons, which could be bad enough, and at times the aerodrome was actually in the fire zone, but what were such things in comparison to the lot of those poor devils on the road?

A voice called across: "Karl Schuster, hallo, Karl Schuster!"

Mechanic Schuster waved excitedly; his face was red with pleasure.

"Hallo! That you, Donisl?" he exclaimed.

"Who is it, Schuster? Who's Donisl?" asked the chief.

"He's my school friend, from my village, sir. We took our first Communion together. Old Donisl!" Schuster could not restrain his joy.

"Off you go!" said the chief. "Don't let the lad shout so. Run along to the captain and ask him to give Donisl leave till tomorrow morning, as a favour to me!"

Schuster darted away like an arrow. The captain halted and listened to him. He returned to report that Donisl would like to bring his friend the corporal, too.

"All right," agreed Olden, "bring all the corporals in the company if you like and if the captain will let them go!"

The captain saw no objection. Seven men came. First they had to have baths; then the chief had a special word with the cook, for they were his guests. He sat with them for a while, and soon they were all speaking such thick Bavarian that none of them could understand the others.

The next morning the chief took them back to their company in a car, for they did not want to leave the clean mechanics' beds too early.

Donisl gave the chief a small wooden figure of a saint as a token of his gratitude. He had carved it when he spent his last leave in Mittenwald and carried it about with him ever since.

CHAPTER XXI

Early in August, 1918, came the order to retreat. All formations were to retire to the huge German reserve positions which the sappers had built up unmolested behind the front lines. All the experience of four years of war were put into them, and they were supposed to be impregnable.

All day and all night long regiments marched on the road flanking the aerodrome. An immense column of emaciated grey figures passed. It was their duty to defend this territory and continue to devastate the battered countryside which resembled a wilderness. They were starved and wizened; their hearts were seared. They were hard and taciturn. War had become their trade.

The German civil authorities gave the local population of this newly-threatened area three hours to evacuate their houses. The poor people migrated eastwards, taking with them only the barest necessities. There were greybeards, women and children; some had a cow or a horse with them. Dogs with hanging ears trotted beside them; wagons, hand-carts and perambulators carried the remains of their household goods.

All day and all night long this procession passed along the road.

All day and all night long there was another procession of soldiers, lorries and guns.

Above: AN OBSERVER EQUIPPED WITH PARACHUTE, JUMPING
FROM A BALLOON ATTACKED BY ENEMY AIRCRAFT
Below: THE BALLOON'S OBSERVER LANDS

Often enough the greybeards, women and children had to take refuge in the ditches by the roadside, for the army had the right of way and needed much space. They did not even curse their fate; they only burst into frequent fits of weeping—and did not know they had wept.

The Staffel of the brown Fokkers also prepared to retreat. The shells of the enemy artillery fell ever more thickly. They tore deep holes in the aerodrome; they tore gaps in the columns marching along the road. But the gaps soon closed up and the huge stream of men rolled onwards.

Olden and his Staffel shared their new station with a section of field aircraft. Unending columns of lorries rolled into it, bringing crates of tools, materials and supplies. The American bomber and a reserve Fokker were to be fetched later on.

The English fire increased in severity, but the chief and his nine pilots took off safely.

When they reached the new aerodrome, there was a roll-call of the mechanics. It elicited the fact that Baumann was missing. They called him again; they looked for him. But no one could find Baumann. The chief waited patiently; his Baumann must be somewhere about.

"Chief!" The prince shook him. "Chief, stop dozing! The English shells! Wake up, man!"

"Yes——?" said the chief.

"I've borrowed a two-seater Rumpler from the field section; we'll go back and have a look on the old 'drome," suggested Steffen.

Olden, the prince and Steffen flew back. The chief was in the two-seater. A huge pillar of fire showed him the way back.

Eight of the ten hangars were in a blaze. They circled round their old aerodrome. The American bomber and the reserve Fokker stood burning before the doors of Hangar 9.

A figure reeled out of the petrol magazine, carrying a pitch-torch. It ran a few steps, fell, rose with some difficulty and ran on. Then the petrol magazine went up with a terrific roar. The man with the torch was miraculously uninjured; he ran on, reeling towards the oil magazine. He was Baumann.

The chief flew down to the ground and landed his machine with a short taxi. "Baumann! Baumann!" he roared with all the strength of his lungs.

Baumann stared at his chief with glazed eyes and ran up to the taxiing machine. He held on to the observer's seat with one hand and on to a strut with the other and was dragged along by the machine until the chief succeeded at last in hoisting him in and pushing him down into the seat behind him with many oaths. With some difficulty Olden pulled his machine off the ground on the brink of a shell-hole; then the three machines turned homewards and landed safe and sound a few minutes later.

After which there was a regular Bavarian thunderstorm. Baumann's sole excuse was: "The swine are not going to get our machines and supplies!"

"But I gave no orders to destroy them!" shouted the chief. "And you've been drinking again! You're tight and you nearly blew yourself up!"

Baumann's mighty hands trembled. "Herr Lieutenant! Herr Lieutenant!"

"Be quiet! I'll have to punish you, Baumann!"

". . . But those swine aren't going to——"

Silence. Then the chief: "Sleep it off first, and we'll look into the business tomorrow!"

Chapter XXII

The changes of aerodrome grew more frequent. The Staffel found nowhere to rest.

At the end of October the Flanders autumn sent its fogs. A closed blanket of dirty grey clouds hung at 200 metres, and the wind tore fluttering swathes from its edges. The pilots called this sort of weather "the laundry" Their visibility was limited to something less than 500 metres.

The front line changed every day. Spying eyes saw the flat-brimmed English or American helmets rising out of trenches which had contained the round German ones the day before.

Every day there was heavy fighting in the air. The Jagdstaffel pushed along the trenches at 20 metres height—where were the friends and where the foes?

The fights were bitter ones, for it seemed as if everyone wanted to put forth his last reserves of energy. English reconnaissance machines harassed the German retreat wherever they could. The numerical superiority of the enemy increased from day to day. Eight to one were the usual odds now. The English and Americans fought ruthlessly, for they had inexhaustible reserves of men and materials.

The brown Fokkers fought as they had never fought before. The pilots hardly slept; they hardly ate; they just flew and fought or changed their aerodrome. And with them went their mechanics.

The never-ending stream of regiments still flowed on. But no new men came to join them. Likewise it often happened that men who went home on leave did not return to the front.

On November 1st and 2nd all available machines were concentrated in the northernmost corner of Flanders. Heavy bombers, scout and reconnaissance machines stood ready to take off.

A huge air raid on England had been planned. It was a raid which would destroy everything that could be destroyed. It was to be a work of destruction on such a colossal scale that it would far exceed anything hitherto done in this war. But it remained only a plan.

For a movement had commenced which no power in the world could stem. It commenced with hopes which were first only thoughts. Later on they were uttered, first between one man and another, then in larger gatherings, and finally they were spoken openly to all—an armistice—the desire for peace.

Lieutenant Olden was well aware of these rumours, but they were no concern of his as long as they did not materialise into facts. The Staffel followed his example and went on fighting.

On November 8th the chief was summoned to H.Q. "He's gone to get details of the raid on England!" said the pilots. But he returned on the 9th, with a face white as a sheet and staring eyes. His sword-knot was missing; his uniform and his right shoulder-strap were torn. He looked to be fifty-six years old instead of twenty-six.

He left his horrified comrades standing, walked into the office as if in a trance and wrote out the following statement: "On my way back from H.Q. I was held up by a sergeant in command of infantrymen wearing red armlets and ordered to remove my swordknot, cockade and shoulder straps. When I refused, the men made a physical assault on me. In my own defence I drew my Browning, fired and wounded the sergeant in the arm."

TAKING BOMBS ON BOARD A GERMAN FIGHTER MACHINE.
NOTE THE SIGNAL LIGHTS BEHIND THE OBSERVER'S SEAT
AND THE HAND GRENADES IN THE RACK.

Then he ordered the whole Staffel to muster. Eight pilots, seventy-eight others—the mechanics, clerks and cooks, with the foremen and the armoury master obeyed the summons—and Olden faced them.

"Comrades, the politicians of the belligerent powers have ordered an armistice!" The chief spoke very clearly, slowly and deliberately. "I herewith resign the leadership of Jagdstaffel 356. You must choose from your ranks a council of four which is to take the Staffel home and await further orders from G.H.Q. Works foreman, ask your mechanics to make their choice."

Eighty-six men remained silent. They had lost their voices. They had lost their reason.

Mierdl touched the chief's arm gently. "Chief?—chief——?" he repeated. But he seemed to be talking to a very sick man.

Eighty-six men stared at their Lieutenant Olden. They heard him continue:

"By permission of the Dutch Government the Staffel will fly through Holland to Krefeld, and then up the Rhine to Mainz."

"And then?" asked Kussin.

"That is all I know, except that G.H.Q. returned to Germany yesterday."

The works foreman stepped forward. "The mechanics do not want any new leaders. The Herr Lieutenant is our leader," he announced.

Olden looked closely up and down the long ranks of the seventy-eight mechanics. And then: "All men of the same opinion one step forward!"

Click-clack! Seventy-eight mechanics took one step forward in closed ranks.

The telephone orderly came hurrying from the house. He ran as if his life was at stake. In his hand he held a paper, which he waved.

"Herr Lieutenant! Herr Lieutenant!" he called from afar.

The man's high-pitched, quavering voice turned all eyes towards the paper he held.

Olden read the telephonic communication. He took a long time reading it.

Eighty-six men saw the gleam of madness in his eyes when he looked up.

He tried to say something. "Chief——?" said a comrade for the third time in warning tones.

Olden read aloud: "The German Republic has been proclaimed in Berlin. His Majesty the Emperor is on his way to a neutral country."

Eighty-six men were silent. They were perplexed and helpless. Then a shot resounded in the midst of their silence. They saw the chief sink to his knees, his hand still grasping the Browning. A small, round hole appeared in his forehead!

The pilots and mechanics sprang forward. The chief lay still on the ground. His comrades looked into the poor eyes that seemed to be asking for help and advice.

Baumann stooped and picked up the chief's cap.

Chapter XXIII

All day and all night long the troops marched along the road. Some sang as they passed; others were tired and silent. All through the day and night regiment after regiment passed. The road echoed with the trot of horse-hoofs and the rumble of lorries. They all wanted to go home now.

All day and all night long pilots relieved one another every two hours in the guard of honour that kept watch by the chief. The mechanics fashioned a coffin, and this time it was the last one.

They made the brown Fokkers serviceable for the last time. Then they piled themselves on to the lorries. With the works foreman as their leader, they drove through Holland to Krefeld. They were to meet the pilots there two days later.

The pilots chose a new leader. Hamann, the youngest of them all, was to take them into Germany. All the Staffel's machines carried long black streamers.

The brown Fokkers took off on the morning of November 13th. They flew in battle formation. Hamann headed the V formed by the others; in their midst was a spare L.V.G., with the leader's streamers floating from it. It carried the chief's coffin. They flew over a land that was uncannily silent. The swarms of returning soldiers were thinning out, and not a single shot had been fired for four days.

They flew over the last trenches when they reached the Dutch-Belgian frontier, and then there were fields, meadows, canals and little villages—Holland. And then came a broad river—the Rhine. Slanting away on the left there lay a town—Krefeld.

They circled over the town and found the aerodrome and its landing-mark. As previously arranged, all but two of the Fokkers went down.

No sooner had they landed than a deputation from the local garrison hastened up. They introduced themselves as the local Soldiers' Council and summoned the pilots to hand over their machines at once.

Hamann replied that he was under orders to take the Staffel to Mainz. The Soldiers' Council grew more insistent.

Hamann fired the red signal light of warning. The prince, who had been circling over the aerodrome, fired a short warning burst from his machine-guns. The Soldiers' Council fled.

The others landed without further trouble. They took in fresh petrol unmolested and resumed their journey up the Rhine.

Rain fell. It was cold.

On Mainz aerodrome stood the deserted machines of a Jagdstaffel which had been stationed in the Verdun area. The pilots had already left.

Baumann and a number of the mechanics met them in the evening. After some trouble they secured a couple of wagons to take the chief's coffin to his home in Bavaria. All the pilots and some of the mechanics wanted to accompany it.

Baumann apologised for his absent comrades. "They have gone home; they said they couldn't all come."

Hamann was forced to remain behind to await the orders of which the chief had spoken.

They bought the finest wreaths they could find in the town and then took leave of one another.

GROUP OF JASTA 35B PILOTS TAKEN AT THE END OF THE WAR, 11 NOVEMBER 1918.

From left to right: Ltn Walderberer, Uffz Hensel, Uffz Werneburg, Uffz Meyer, Uffz Marx, Uffz Gassl, Vfe Hofmann, Ltn Ach, Ltn Karl Beyschlag, Gfr Brey, Ltn Rudolf Stark, Ltn Rudolf Hess (who was later to be Hitler's Deputy Führer), Ltn Carl Kranz, Ltn Heinrich Stoer, Ltn Helmo Ludovici, Ltn Hauft (OzbV). *Photo courtesy of Norman Franks.*

Chapter XXIV

Hamann remained behind in Mainz. His only companion on the huge aerodrome was a captain, who attended to the scanty business of the day. Every now and then a clerk came out from the town and sat forlornly in the spacious office.

All wore civilian dress now. Hamann asked his mother to send him a suit, because he had not enough money to buy a new one. The only good suit he had at home was his confirmation one, which had grown far too tight for him.

The Fokkers stood all forlorn on the aerodrome, waiting for the Englishmen who were to take them over.

The captain's vigilance frustrated an attempt to burn them. "Don't do it, comrade," he warned Hamann. "We shall only have to pay heavy indemnities for them!"

Hamann never went into the town. He slept, ate, stood by his machines and waited. He was too deeply rooted in the past to become conscious of the present, while the future was something strange and uncertain.

One morning twenty English machines were there. All round the aerodrome stood American tanks. They had arrived overnight.

Hamann went up to an officer of high rank. "Are you the leader of this formation?" he asked in German. The American waved to his interpreter.

Hamann repeated his question. "As deputy-leader of Jagdstaffel 356 I am authorised to hand over to you eight Fokkers and one

L.V.G." The officer bowed slightly and thanked him.

Hamann saw the English pilots eyeing the German machines and comparing them with their own. He turned to the interpreter. "I hope I may be allowed to go now," he said. The man assented.

Hamann went past his Fokkers and strode on through the midst of the English and American soldiers and tanks. He walked with a slight stoop. His dark confirmation suit, which was far too tight for him, made his appearance almost ridiculous.

A clear sharp word of command in the English language made him turn round. He saw all the officers, pilots and soldiers raise their hands to their helmets and salute him; he saw the sentries at the entrance to the aerodrome present arms as he passed them. They all saluted the last pilot of the brown Fokkers.

The vision remained with him as he wandered along the road leading to the town. Before him lay the world, home and peace.